Rawfully Good

RAWFULLY GOOD

'Living' Flavours of Southeast Asia

Diana von Cranach

RIVER
BOOKS

First published and distributed in 2010 by
River Books Co., Ltd
396 Maharaj Road, Tatien, Bangkok 10200
Tel: (66) 2 225-4963, 2 225-0139, 2 622-1900
Fax: (66) 2 225-3861
Email: order@riverbooksbk.com
www.riverbooksbk.com

ISBN: 978 190 45621 22
Editor: Narisa Chakrabongse
Production: Paisarn Piammattawat
Design: Peter Cope

Printed and bound in Thailand by Sirivatana Interprint Co., Ltd.

Contents

How to use this book

Please remember that the recipes in this book are only supposed to be guidelines and that most of the ingredients mentioned can be substituted by produce that is locally available.

Be prepared to experiment with new and exciting ingredients and please do not be intimidated by the long list of unknown ones that you might read about in this book for the first time.

Learn to adjust and balance the amounts of herbs and spices used in the recipes to your taste.

Use the recipes to prepare delicious, healthy alternatives to heavy, cooked or processed food and to help you to introduce 'living' dishes into your diet.

Find the time to source the freshest and best possible produce from farmer's markets and buy 'organically' grown fruit and vegetables whenever possible.

Discover the ethnic food shops in your area to find some of the more unusual ingredients mentioned in this book.

Research 'living' food online. One of the most helpful and comprehensive websites is www.sunfoodtraveler.com

Contact me if you need help or futher information about ingredients or the use of substitute herbs, spices, fruits or vegetables – diana@puriganesha.com

Foreword Chris Miller, Executive Chef COMO Resorts

I first met the incredibly energetic and always inspiring Diana in 2006 at a New Year's Eve party in the sleepy town of Ubud. Within moments we were deep in conversation, discussing food, restaurants, hotels and everything relating to cooking until the early hours of 2007.

Over the next four years I have watched Diana experiment with, create, promote and just simply 'live' all manner of things raw. From her amazing menus at Puri Ganesha, to guest promotions around the world, producing delicious retail products and cookbooks, Diana has carved a niche for herself by bringing new flavours and ideas to 'raw' dining tables everywhere.

Diana and I decided to collaborate to prepare 'living' versions of the Indonesian reistafel and reinvent traditional local recipes. We wanted to create something that would be unique, healthy, fun and most importantly, full of local flavours. We were happy to discover that most of the fruits, herbs and vegetables that we had been using regularly in our respective resort kitchens lent themselves perfectly to a 'living' style of preparation. We could replace braising, deep frying, shrimp paste and fish sauce with the amazing aromas of lemon basil, turmeric, galangal, the moist crunch of palm hearts, the sweetness of mangoes, pineapples and all the other wild and wonderful local produce for good measure!

Being lucky enough to live in the tropics of Southeast Asia allows us to source so much locally, ensuring that the body keeps healthy, the environment is more protected and the local community supported.

These are important factors to keep in mind when using this book as many of the ingredients will not only be completely unknown to readers but will be impossible to obtain in other parts of the world. This culinary knowledge is fantastic for interest's sake but Diana's intention and the reason for the book was not only to create unusual 'living' dishes, but to inspire readers to keep the basic Southeast Asian flavours while trying to be creative and use all the fresh, seasonal, local and preferably organically grown produce available wherever they may be – the ingredients will be far fresher and have a minimal carbon footprint.

The recipes in this book will encourage readers to think about 'living' food in a completely new light and differently delicious way. Instead of dehydrating, Diana loves to awaken the palette with new flavours and serve only the freshest of vegetable, herb, spice, fruit and nut combinations prepared *à la minute*, to be eaten immediately.

Although many of the ingredients may surprise and even confuse readers at times, experimentation and substitution are fun as well as being educational and this book provides a basis for creating the healthiest, most fabulous-tasting, vibrant and quite addictively, 'rawfully good' Southeast Asian Food imaginable.

Introduction

'Foods that have ripened and been brought to a state of maturity by nature cannot consistently be called 'raw.' The origin of this word was the effort to describe something that was unfinished, that was crude, that was rough, or in some way objectionable. These things are finished, ready for use; they are perfect, they are not raw, they are done; and when they are cooked they are undone.'
'Uncooked Foods & How to Use Them' Eugene Christian, New York, 1924

This book is a way of introducing 'living food', using recipes from Southeast Asia, to everyone who would like to eat more delicious, nutritious food and experiment with many new, exciting and exotic ingredients.

I hope that this book can be an inspiration to anyone who loves trying new flavours. Although many of the ingredients used in this book cannot be found outside Asia and many only in particular regions, this does not mean that they have to be sourced religiously by readers who live in other parts of the world. Some of the ingredients can be found in health food shops, 'organic' departments of supermarket chains or Asian grocers who sell an amazing selection of fresh, imported Asian products with a huge carbon footprint. Buy only basic imported ingredients at the outset, before trying to replace them with other interesting, seasonal, fresh, local and if possible 'organic' produce grown by farmers nearer to home.

Increasing numbers of people all over the world are becoming aware of the dangers of eating over processed, homogenized and genetically modified foods and beginning to question what is actually added to the large amounts of convenience dishes that they buy every day. Making a radical decision to change to a diet made up largely of 'living' food can be an exciting, healthy and exhilarating adventure. Contrary to general opinions, 'living foodies' are neither a gang of ageing hippies nibbling nuts nor a fanatic group of top earners fussing over a long list of strange sounding ingredients known only to a chosen few.

Before planning a transition to eating 'living' food, there are three things to be considered: more time and effort are required to source the best possible ingredients, preparation times can be longer and an initial investment to buy the equipment needed to help prepare 'living' food (see Utensils) is necessary. On the other hand, turning off the stove, putting away the pans and throwing out the microwave is actually much easier than anyone can possibly imagine.

Trying to follow a purely 'living' food diet is not recommended for everyone and in some cases can be dangerous, so every individual has to experiment and find out what feels comfortable. An ideal and balanced 'living' diet should include a ratio of

30% to 70% raw to cooked food. 'Living' food does not include dairy, animal products or processed food of any kind. No ingredient should ever be heated above 118 degrees to ensure that the natural enzymes remain intact, so boosting the body's immune system to avert disease and help digestion. The positive health benefits of eating 'living' food are incalculable.

Making 'living' food for everyday can be a bit of a creative challenge at the outset because a great deal of care and thought are required. Ingredients have to be nutritionally balanced, include different textures, interesting flavours and the way in which the dishes are presented should be especially tempting and appeal to all the senses. Definitely not just a case of opening a bag of salad, finding or taking the time to prepare 'living' food, as well as enjoying experimenting with new and very different ways of combining ingredients is very important – try to be passionate but never fanatical about what you are trying to create!

The most successful recipes are usually those that do not adhere to any exact measurements, but have a cleverly orchestrated and exciting balance of flavours and textures, not forgetting that every individual has their own preferred tastes. Because fresh produce and ingredients easily available around the world will have different levels of the six most important of these: sweetness, acidity, sourness, saltiness, bitterness and astringency, it is important to keep experimenting with the recipes in this book, find satisfaction in discovering new combinations and to have fun working on plating and presentation.

Being lucky enough to live in Bali where a copious array of wonderful and unusual ingredients are available all year round, I decided to create my unique kind of purely Southeast Asian 'rawfully good' living food, using local recipes but removing the animal ingredients and adjusting the flavours accordingly.

The main difficulty to overcome when transitioning to more of a 'living' food diet is a purely social one. Invitations to dinner parties, lunches or afternoon teas can present a huge challenge and trying to adhere to a completely 'living' diet while keeping up an active social life is practically impossible. There is no reason to panic, just eat cooked food, drink alcohol in moderation and cleanse your system with a few days of purely 'living' food afterwards.

Personally, I am not a fanatical 'raw foodie' by any means and often succumb to more than the occasional negative food or alcohol 'binge'. But eating this kind of 'living' food most of the time gives me astonishing amounts of energy, a heightened sense of taste, of smell and as an added bonus, it seems to help combat many of the aches and pains usually associated with the ageing process.

Bali

Puri Ganesha Villas, Pemuteram

Since the beginning of the 20th century the old cliché depicting Bali as the ultimate paradise island and holiday destination still remains unchanged, despite horrendous terrorist bombings and the onslaught of mass tourism. The trend to develop further already overbuilt, mundane Seminyak into a purely party, shopping and fine dining zone for villa owners and fun-seeking tourists marches on relentlessly. In Ubud, Bali's cultural heart, traditional Balinese handicraft sellers are being taken over by tastefully refurbished small shops with Japanese or Javanese owners. But, in spite of the apparent westernisation, just head out into the countryside or venture down one of the narrow alleys behind those endless rows of shops and find that the Balinese – cultural chameleons and natural linguists every one – are still managing to keep a careful balance between making a living from tourism and practicing the complicated religious rituals according to traditions handed down through many generations.

Like so many before me, I fell under Bali's spell when I arrived in the early 1980s and, immediately deciding to make Bali my permanent home sometime in the future, I bought a piece of desolate beachfront land in a then completely unknown fishing community in the northwest corner of the island, four hours from the airport. Friends and family considered me to be certifiable and there were many difficult times later when I nearly believed it myself. In 1996 after a 22-year marriage fell apart, I bought a one way ticket to Bali at the age of 48, taking only a packing case, suitcase and the equivalent of US $200.00! Without having any idea what I had got myself into and with no money to invest at all, my idea was to develop the land I had bought and build a very small personally-run hotel. The following years were extremely difficult and filled with many sad, sometimes soul-destroying experiences.

Gusti my Balinese husband and I married in 1998. We lived at home in the village with his parents for a time and, as part of a huge extended family, I took part in all the religious rituals of passage, studied how to use herbs, spices and medicinal leaves, and learnt about the significance of the daily offerings and the basics of Balinese food

from my mother-in-law. The strangest thing for me as a foreigner was being accepted as a fully-fledged member of the extended family community without question.

This knowledge of Bali seen through our two very different cultural backgrounds is what we personally like to give to our guests. They can learn how to pray at one of the many famous temples nearby, more about everyday life on the island, join a family ceremony, have lunch at the family home in the village, eat at some of the best local lean-to cafés with us, prepare authentic north Bali fare, shop for beautiful and very different local handicrafts or take a day trip to nearby Java.

Because I love experimenting with the hundreds of locally-grown ingredients that are readily available, Puri Ganesha has become a food haven and we are one of only a few hotels worldwide to offer a purely 'living' food as well as an organic menu. We have no set mealtimes, do not serve red meat and because over 95% of our produce is sourced locally, we are happy to take guests with us on our spice, chocolate and vanilla buying sprees to our local suppliers. My chefs are untrained local villagers who effortlessly serve our guests the tastiest, freshest and most interesting food possible!

In the last twenty years, prosperity through tourism has come to our carefully developed little fishing village. Pemuteran appeals to an increasing number of intrepid guests searching for a more peaceful side of Bali. They are undaunted by the long but very beautiful trip over the central mountains to reach this isolated location with no night life or shopping. Our Bali is of course no longer the intact, pristine paradise that many expect to find, but we hope that by taking guests to discover little-known mountain villages, spice farms and moss-covered temples as well as helping them to try some of the best local food on the island, they can catch a glimpse of Balinese life and take valuable and lasting memories home with them.

Puri Ganesha Villas, Desa Pemuteran, North Bali, Indonesia
Telephone: +62 362 94766 F: + 62 362 93433
Email: gusti@puriganesha.com Web: www.puriganesha.com

Indonesian 'living' *soto* soup with all the extras

Serves 2

Ingredients
1 tbs vegan, low salt stock powder
2 tbs fresh turmeric, chopped
1 tbs fresh galangal, chopped
1 tbs fresh garlic, chopped
2 lime leaves, shredded
Inside of 2 lemongrass stems finely chopped
4 shallots
2 cloves of garlic
½ tsp coriander seed
½ tsp white peppercorns
1 tbs palm sugar
Sea salt to taste
200-250 mls water
1 tbs spicy raw nuts (see *Tasty Extras*)
1 tbs crispy fried onions

Grind or blend the above ingredients together to make a paste. Adjust the seasoning, add the water, mix well and gently heat. Spoon the soup into warm bowls, top liberally with crispy potatoes or onions (see *Tasty Extras*) and serve with the following extras: lemon basil leaves, tomatoes, shredded cabbage, beansprouts, shitake mushrooms, carrots, tempe or tofu cut into cubes, chilli and tomato sambal, chopped chili in tamari sauce or whatever you like!

Avocado & palm heart appetizer

Serves 2

Ingredients
1 avocado per person, chopped or sliced
1 cup palm heart, finely sliced
3 shallots, finely sliced
1 orange, peeled & segments sliced
2 large red radishes
8 stinkbeans, sliced
1 tbs mint, finely chopped
1 tsp fresh ginger, finely chopped
½ or 1 large red chilli, deseeded, very finely chopped
2 inside stems of lemongrass, finely sliced

Dressing
1 tbs raw honey
2 tbs lime juice
1 tsp or more sesame oil
Sea salt to taste

Prepare all the ingredients before chopping the avocado. Make the dressing, adjust the seasoning and add all the ingredients together, mixing well.

Singaraja style vegetables with spicy tomato sauce

Serves 2

Ingredients

50g each red & green spinach leaves, chopped
100g ferntips, tips only cut into small pieces
4 baby aubergines sliced & soaked in salty water
   for 20 minutes then drained and dried
50g white or other cabbage, thinly sliced
½ cucumber, peeled, deseeded & quartered

Singaraja tomato sauce

3 ripe tomatoes, chopped
3 large red chillies, deseeded & chopped
1 small red chilli, deseeded & chopped
2 garlic cloves, chopped
1 tsp palm sugar or to taste
Juice ½ limo or lime with extra salt
½-1 tsp sea salt
1 tsp virgin coconut oil

Blend or pound the above together to make a smooth paste. Prepare and mix the vegetables for the salad. Just before serving, add the tomato sauce. Serve at once.

Baby aubergine, tomato & herb tower with fresh coconut & chilli pesto

Serves 2

Ingredients

100g baby Asian aubergines
100g mixed mushrooms
3 large tomatoes, sliced
4 shallots, sliced
50g carrots, thinly sliced
30g sprouts, any kind
50g chopped green vegetables of choice
1 lg red chilli, deseeded & chopped
1 tbs spring onions, green tops only
1 tbs Thai holy basil leaves, shredded
2 tbs coriander leaves, left whole
½ tsp black pepper
1 tsp sea salt or to taste
1 tsp crispy shallots (see *Tasty Extras*)
2 tbs spicy nuts (see *Tasty Extras*)
2 tbs freshly grated or dried coconut

Finely slice the baby aubergines and sprinkle with salt.
Leave for 30 minutes, then drain off the water and pat dry.
Slice the tomatoes and discard the seeds, season with salt
& pepper. Place in a strainer over a bowl to drain off
excess liquid. Carefully clean and slice the mushrooms
and mix with lime juice and the chopped herbs, salt and
pepper to taste. Prepare the remaining ingredients. Stack
everything in alternate layers. Garnish with coriander
leaves and crispy onions and sprinkle the coconut around.

Chilli pesto
2 tbs Thai holy basil leaves
1 tsp Chinese celery leaves, chopped
1 large red chilli, deseeded & finely chopped
2 tbs coconut or good salad oil
1 tbs lime juice
Sea salt & pepper to taste

Blend the above ingredients together and set aside.

To serve
Stack layers of all the ingredients, finishing off with a layer
of mushrooms. Serve immediately at room temperature
with the pesto in a little dish.

North Bali wild herb & petal salad

Serves 2

Ingredients
50g mixed flower petals: we used local bougainville, hibiscus, marigold, pink and white vegetable humming-bird, safflower, frangipani and ylang-ylang but any petals that look and taste good can be used instead.

50g mixed leaves and herbs: we used wild spinach, drumstick tree, vegetable hummingbird, turmeric, Asian clover, chives and shredded lime leaves, or just use whatever is available.

2 shallots, finely sliced

Dressing
¼ fresh mature coconut, grated or
2 tbs dried, grated, unsweetened coconut
2 garlic cloves
1 tsp fresh turmeric, chopped
2 'grates' of fresh nutmeg
1 tbs palm sugar, chopped
10 coriander seeds
1 large red chilli, deseeded & chopped

Blend or pound the dressing ingredients together, adding a little coconut oil or water if it is too thick. Remove stamens from the flowers and pluck into single petals. Mix in carefully with the other ingredients. Just before serving, pour over the dressing and mix well. Serve and eat immediately so that the petals do not have time to wilt.

Tempeh & *gado gado* east-west salad with peanut sauce dressing & chunky peanut sauce

Serves 2

Ingredients
2 thin slices of raw tempeh for each serving, cut horizontally

Spice paste for the tempeh
3 cm fresh turmeric, chopped
4 garlic cloves, chopped
2 shallots, chopped
1 tsp coriander seeds
Sea salt and white pepper to taste
2-3 tbs water

Grind or pound the spices together and check the seasoning. Add water to thin the paste and soak the tempeh slices for 20 mins on each side, ensuring that they are covered by the spice paste water. Pat dry.

Gado-gado east-west salad
50g each sliced cucumber, grated carrots, shredded cabbage, mushrooms, avocado & soy or other sprouts
1 large red chilli, deseeded & chopped
20g each lemon basil leaves & chives
2 stalks Chinese celery, leaves only
Sea salt & white pepper to taste

Peanut Sauce Dressing
3 cups raw peanuts
3 garlic cloves
2 small shallots
1 large red chilli, seeds removed
2 shredded lime leaves
¼ cup palm sugar
1 tsp kecap manis sweet soy sauce (optional)
2 tbs coconut milk mixed with 2 tbs water
1 tsp sea salt to taste

Blend or pound the above ingredients together, adding the coconut milk and water to dilute.

Chunky peanut sauce

100g coarsely ground raw peanuts
1 tbs virgin coconut oil
2 garlic cloves
1 large red chilli, seeds removed
¼ cup palm sugar
Salt & white pepper to taste

Grind or pound the ingredients together & season to taste.

To serve

Toss the salad ingredients with the peanut sauce dressing. Adjust the seasoning. Put one slice of tempeh on a plate, cover with salad, then another slice of tempeh, finishing off with herb topping and spicy peanuts (see *Tasty Extras*). Drizzle the peanut dressing around the tempeh and garnish with greens and more finely shredded lime leaves. Serve and eat immediately so that the petals have no time to wilt, with the pesto in a little dish on the side.

Tempeh handrolls with Asian carrot slaw

Serves 2

Ingredients
1 large block of tempeh, cut horizontally
    into four thin slices
1 tsp coriander seed
3 garlic cloves, chopped
2 tsp fresh turmeric, chopped
1 tsp palm sugar to taste
1 tsp tamari soy sauce
1 tsp sea salt or to taste

Pound or blend the above to make a spice paste, adding
enough water to cover the tempeh slices. Soak them for
1 hour. Remove from the water, drain and gently pat dry.

Wind the tempeh around 4 empty tomato paste tins. Put
in the dehydrator at 100 degrees for 12 hours or until the
tempeh is dry enough to carefully remove the tins. Replace
in the dehydrator to finish drying completely.

Asian slaw
200g carrots, grated
1 tsp coriander seeds
½ tsp black peppercorns
1 tsp raw honey
1 tsp or more of lime juice
Tiny pinch of cumin seeds
2 shallots, sliced
1 small red chilli, deseeded & chopped
2 tsp raw cashews, chopped
2 tbs fresh young coconut, chopped into slivers
½ tsp black sesame seeds
Salt to taste

Just before serving, make the salad, adjust the seasoning
and spoon into the tempeh rolls. Serve immediately
before the tempeh goes soft. Serve with extra slaw.

Cauliflower & vegetable rice

Serves 2

Ingredients
1 medium cauliflower, chopped very finely to resemble 'rice'
2 long green beans, sliced or green peas
2 tbs lemon basil leaves
2 spring onions, chopped
1 small green chilli, deseeded & chopped

Spice paste
1 tsp fresh ginger
1 tsp fresh galangal
1 tsp fresh turmeric
1 tsp fresh kencur
1 tsp palm sugar
1-2 tsp lime juice
1-2 tbs coconut milk
Sea salt to taste

Pound or blend the above together to make a paste and adjust the seasoning. Just before serving add the spice paste to the 'rice' and vegetables. Mix well and adjust the seasoning again. Serve in a decorative form of your choice with a sambal or two (see *Sambals*) and a sprinkling of fresh herbs.

Puri Ganesha special spicy fruit & vegetable salad

Serves 2

In Indonesia, this salad is usually eaten to wake up the senses after an afternoon nap, so getting the balance right between sweet, sour and tangy flavours is most important. Any kind of mixed soft and crunchy fruit and vegetables can be used for this salad.

Ingredients
50g okra, sliced
1 star fruit, sliced
50g strawberries, sliced
¼ pineapple, cut into small pieces
¼ half ripe (just pink) papaya, cut into small pieces
6 rambutan, peeled, stone taken out & chopped
2 small apples, cored & sliced
2 small carrots, peeled & chopped
½ cucumber, peeled, deseeded & sliced
1 tsp dried or fresh jasmine flowers, stamens removed
1 tbs crispy shallots (see *Tasty Extras*)

Palm sugar paste
1 tsp tamarind paste
1 tsp white vinegar (optional)
50g palm sugar
1 small red chilli, deseeded
½ tsp sea salt or to taste
Make the paste & adjust the seasoning

Prepare all the salad ingredients and mix together with the palm sugar paste and adjust the seasoning before serving.

Ting-ting 'living' Balinese peanut brittle

Makes approximately 10 pieces

Ingredients
75g raw cashews, soaked overnight
75g raw peanuts, soaked for 3 hours
10g sesame seed (unhulled if possible) soaked for 1 hour
100g palm sugar
Pinch of sea salt

Drain the nuts and seeds very well. When dry, blend or
pound them together to make a thick, chunky paste. Add
the palm sugar and salt and adjust the seasoning again.
Form the paste into a roll 6 cm in diameter and slice into
rounds. Dehydrate at 115 degrees for about 15 hours or
until dry to the touch. Turn over carefully and dry for
another 10 hours or until the biscuits are dry but soft.

Rawfully Good / Puri Ganesha Villas

Bali superfood no-sugar treats

Makes 8 to 10 pieces

Ingredients
50g raw cashew nuts
50g goji berries
30g raw cocoa beans
50g raw cocoa butter, finely grated
30g orange zest

Chop the first three ingredients into very small pieces
then mix into the grated cocoa butter together with the
orange zest. Form into small balls and keep in the fridge.
Use within 7 days.

Five Balinese *sambals*

Makes 2 portions

Sambals can be served as dips for raw vegetables, tempeh
or crackers. Most of the recipes are traditional but some
are just put together from tasty local ingredients. All the
tastes – sweet, sour, salty – can be adjusted accordingly!

TOMATO SAMBAL

1 large garlic clove
1 large ripe tomato
1 small red chilli & ½ large red chilli, seeded & chopped
into small pieces
1 tsp palm sugar
¼ tsp sea salt
1 tsp virgin coconut oil
Juice of ½ a tiny limo or ½ lime
Grind together and make a paste out of the first four
ingredients. Add the sugar and salt to taste, then the virgin
coconut oil and lime juice. Mix well just before serving.

RED ONION SAMBAL

4 small red shallots
½ large red chili seeded & very finely sliced
½ tsp sea salt
½ tsp palm sugar to taste
1 tsp virgin coconut oil
Juice of ¼ of a tiny limo or ½ lime
Mix the all the ingredients together, adjust the seasoning
just before serving.

GINGER FLOWER SAMBAL

1 finely sliced ginger flower bud, outer leaves removed
2 small red shallots, finely sliced
1 large red chilli, seeded & finely sliced
½ tsp palm sugar or more to taste
Juice of ¼ of a tiny limo or ½ lime
Prepare all the ingredients, mix together and adjust the
seasoning just before serving.

Rawfully Good / Puri Ganesha Villas

LEMONGRASS SAMBAL

2 sticks lemongrass very finely sliced, outer leaves removed
2 small red shallots, finely sliced
½ large red chilli seeded & very finely sliced
Juice of ½ a tiny limo or ½ lime
½ tsp sea salt
Prepare all the above and adjust the seasoning.
Mix the ingredients together well just before serving.

TEMPEH SAMBAL

¼ block of fresh tempeh
1 large garlic clove
1 large chilli & 1 small chilli, seeded & chopped
1 tsp virgin coconut oil
Juice of ¼ of a tiny limo or ½ lime
Pinch ground white pepper
Salt to taste
Grind or blend the first four ingredients into a paste,
then add the coconut oil, limo, sugar and salt to taste just
before serving.

Tomato sambal   Red onion sambal   Ginger flower sambal

Lemongrass sambal   Tempeh sambal

Six Javanese *sambals*

Makes 2 portions

LONG BEAN SAMBAL
100g long beans
1 cm kencur
1 cm galangal
½ cm turmeric
1 clove garlic
1 tsp palm sugar
2 small red chillies
½ tsp sea salt
1 tbs crispy onions

Cut the long beans into slices. Set aside. Pound the other ingredients together into a paste, then add the long beans and mix well. Before serving, top with crispy onions.

BABY AUBERGINE SAMBAL
50g baby aubergines
2 cloves garlic
2 large red chilli, seeded & chopped
½ tsp sea salt
Juice of ½ tiny limo or ½ lime
2 shallots, finely sliced
1 tsp palm sugar
1 tsp palm sugar
1 tbs virgin coconut oil

Slice the aubergines very finely and sprinkle with salt. Leave for 20 minutes, wash and drain. Pound the chilli and garlic together adding salt to taste. Add the aubergines and sliced shallots, mix carefully before adding the virgin coconut oil.

SPICY SWEET SOY SAMBAL
4 tbs kecap manis sweet soy sauce
3 small red chillies, chopped, seeds left in this time
1 tbs crispy onions

Before serving, add chili and onions to the sweet soy sauce.

Rawfully Good / Puri Ganesha Villas

STINKBEAN SAMBAL

20g stinkbeans, finely chopped
3 cherry tomatoes, chopped
1 large red chilli, seeded & chopped
1 large garlic clove
2 shallots, chopped
Juice of ¼ tiny limo or ½ lime
Sea salt to taste
1 tsp virgin coconut oil

Remove stinkbeans from their pod and slice finely.
Pound the remaining ingredients together to make a paste.
Add the coconut oil and adjust the seasoning, then add
the beans.

SESAME & CASHEW SAMBAL

50g sesame seeds
50g raw cashew nuts
2 cherry tomatoes, chopped
1 small red chilli, seeded & chopped
1 large red chilli, seeded & chopped
1 tbs palm sugar
1 tsp tamarind paste
¼ tsp freshly ground black pepper
6 leaves Thai sweet lemon basil
Salt to taste

Pound all the ingredients together and add salt to taste.
If the paste is too thick, add a little water coconut milk.

GREEN SAMBAL

2 cloves garlic
2 cm kencur
5 pieces green chilli, seeded & chopped
4 pieces green tomato
½ tsp sea salt
½ tsp white pepper
1 tsp palm sugar
Juice of 1 lime
Leaves from 3 stalks of lemon basil.

Pound all the ingredients together, adding lemon basil
leaves just before serving.

Four fresh vegetable & spice *sambals*

Makes 2 portions

YOUNG PAPAYA SAMBAL

100g green papaya
2 small chillies, seeded & chopped
2 shallots, finely sliced
1 tsp fresh ginger, peeled & chopped
Juice of ½ lime
Sea salt & palm sugar to taste
Coarsely grate the green papaya and set aside.
Make the spice paste with the other ingredients.
Just before serving mix in the papaya and sliced shallots
and adjust the seasoning.

KENCUR SAMBAL

3 small red chillies, seeded & chopped
3 large red chillies, seeded & chopped
3 tbs kencur, grated
4 candlenuts, chopped
1 tsp tamarind paste
2 lime leaves, finely sliced
Juice ½ lime
Sea salt & palm sugar to taste
Pound all the above together to make a paste, adding more
water or lime juice if the paste is too thick.

Young papaya *sambal*   Kencur *sambal*

COCONUT SAMBAL

½ coconut, brown skin removed
1 large red chilli, seeded & chopped
1 small red chilli, seeded & chopped
1 large lime leaf, finely sliced
1 garlic clove
1 cm turmeric, chopped
2 shallots, finely sliced
2 tbs palm sugar
Zest & juice of ½ lime
Sea salt to taste
1 tsp virgin coconut oil
Grate the coconut. Pound or blend the other ingredients together to make a paste. Add the grated coconut and mix well, adjusting the seasoning just before serving.

COCONUT MILK SAMBAL

2 cloves garlic, chopped
2 shallots chopped
2 small red chillies, chopped
1 tbs kencur, chopped
1 tbs raw peanuts, chopped
Sea salt & palm sugar to taste
1-2 tbs coconut milk
1 tbs freshly grated coconut
Pound or blend all the ingredients together to make a thick paste. Adjust the seasoning and add the grated coconut just before serving.

Coconut *sambal*

Coconut milk *sambal*

Traditional Javanese *jamu*

Serves 2

In Indonesia, drinking *jamu* for health and using herbal
products for beauty are part of daily life and a huge
national industry, little known about outside Indonesia.
Many of these herbal recipes are closely guarded family
secrets passed orally from mother to daughter over
centuries. No one knows exactly where *jamu* came from,
but many of the recipes originated in the courts of Central
Java around 12th century. Hundreds of different remedies
are available at specialist shops all over Indonesia but
freshly made *jamu* is healthier, tastier and more potent
than any shop bought powder.

The following recipe is for a simple, 'cure-all' jamu that
can be quickly prepared from ingredients available at
oriental grocers all over the world.

Ingredients
2 tbs fresh turmeric, peeled & chopped
1 tsp tamarind paste
Juice of 1 lime
2 tbs raw honey
100 mls spring water

Blend the above together, adjust the flavors to suit your
tastebuds and drink regularly for a healthy 'glow'.

Bali

COMO Shambhala Estate, Ubud

U bud has become an international meeting point for those who are trying to recreate the Bali that everyone seems to have in their minds. Not the Bali of beaches, parties and bars, but the Bali of seemingly endless tiers of rice fields ascending into the mountain mist and a culture that revolves around colourful religious ceremonies with complicated rituals in hidden, moss-covered temples.

Artistic tradition has always been part of the celebration of life in Ubud, evolving from making music, dancing, wood and stone carving, traditional pastimes enjoyed after work in the rice fields had been completed for another season.

In the mid 1920s tourism was centered around the Bali Hotel in Denpasar and up in the hills of Ubud, foreign artists such as the German painter, Walter Spies and Dutch artist Rudolf Bonnet were being hosted by Ubud royalty. Later in the 1930s Noel Coward, Charlie Chaplin, Barbara Hutton and other famous names headed up into the hinterland, turning Ubud into one of the most sought after bohemian places in the world to see and be seen.

The Balinese themselves have always been religious, cultural and linguistic chameleons, somehow adapting to dealing with the influx of visitors from all over the world with their different needs and expectations. While also managing to earn a living, they still take all the time in the world to attend to what they do best – their many religious ceremonies.

In the last few years, globalization has reached Ubud. The village has grown into a town, tour buses, restaurants and bars abound and many interesting tiny shops are being pushed out and replaced by larger, glossier ones selling brand names. However, it is still easy to find the real magic of Ubud hidden away behind the rows of shops, so just follow small lanes and venture out into the rice fields which are never far away.

Situated outside Ubud is one of the most publicized hotels in the world, the fabled COMO Shambhala Estate. Built originally by a tai-pan family from Hong Kong, COMO's owner Christina Ong took over the Estate in 2004 and transformed it into a holistic destination committed to improving the wellbeing of famous friends and guests. Food plays an important role here and the Estate's healing programmes and treatments are counterbalanced with diets put together specifically for each individual guest.

In 2006 Executive Chef Chris Miller, Balinese chef Dewa Putra Wijaya and I worked together to offer a series of 'Rawstafel' lunches, serving purely 'rawfully good' food-tasting menus using only locally-sourced, seasonal and naturally-grown produce. Because The Estate and Puri Ganesha are two of the only hotels in the world to offer alternative 'living' food menus, we have put together special three or five night 'Healing Through Food' retreats that combine stays at both places.

The following 10 course 'Rawfully Good' menu that we prepared together at The Estate reflects the cuisines and many of the flavours I discovered in my travels around Southeast Asia.

Contact: COMO Shambhala Estate at Begawan Giri, Ubud, Gianyar 80571
Telephone: +62 361 978 888 Fax:+62 361 978 889
Email: info@cse.comoshambhala.bz Web: www.cse.como.bz

Asinan Javanese fruit & vegetable salad

Serves 2

Ingredients
200g chopped mixed fruit and vegetables such as carrot,
    apple, watermelon, avocado, pineapple, cucumber,
    chayote & melon
1tsp fresh papaya seeds

Dressing
Sea salt to taste
50g tamarind paste
Juice of 1 lime
1 tbs palm sugar
50g fresh ginger, chopped
2 garlic cloves, chopped
2 kaffir lime leaves, shredded
2 inside stems of lemongrass,
finely sliced
20g shallots, chopped
2 large red chillies, deseeded &
finely chopped
1 tbs spicy nuts (see *Tasty Extras*)

Make a dressing with the first four
ingredients and add the other herbs
and spices. Adjust the seasoning to
taste. Prepare the fruit and vegetables
and just before serving mix with
the dressing. Top with herbs and
more spicy nuts.

Palm heart & pineapple soup

Serves 2

Ingredients
50g palm heart, chopped
100 mls pineapple juice
100g young coconut
2 tbs coconut milk
2 shallots, chopped
1 garlic cloves, chopped
1 tbs kencur, chopped
2 small green chilli, deseeded & chopped

Blend all the above ingredients together just before
serving. Adjust the flavours and serve immediately.
Serve immediately with a slice of heart of palm topped
with some chopped pineapple and a small piece of green
chilli.

Tropical mango salad

Serves 2

Ingredients
50g ripe mango, chopped
100g half ripe mango, sliced
100g half ripe papaya, sliced
½ tsp green peppercorns, crushed
50g long beans, finely chopped
50g cherry tomatoes, quartered
1 tbs shallots, finely sliced
2 tbs coriander leaves, left whole
1 tbs spearmint leaves, chopped
1 tbs sweet Thai basil, chopped
1 sm red chilli, deseeded & chopped
1 tbs spicy nuts (see *Tasty Extras*)
1 tbs crispy onions (see *Tasty Extras*)

Chop and slice all the ingredients and combine
carefully just before serving.

Dressing
Juice of 2 limes
2 tbs coriander roots, chopped
1-2 tbs palm sugar, chopped
1 garlic clove
1 small green chilli, deseeded & chopped
1 small red chilli, deseeded & chopped
Sea salt to taste

Chop and prepare all the ingredients and mix well.
Adjust the seasoning.

To serve
Check the seasoning of the dressing again before mixing
with the other ingredients. Top each serving with
some spicy nuts and crispy onions (see *Tasty Extras*).
Serve immediately with more coriander leaves on the top.

Lao herb salad

Serves 2

Ingredients
100g of any mixed herbs and leaves that are available, but not forgetting lots of dill
    We used:
1 flower or ginger flower stem, finely sliced Thai holy basil, Thai sweet basil, spearmint, chives, coriander, rice paddy herb, tumeric leaf, kencur leaf, drumstick leaves & young tamarind leaves
Inside part of 2 stems of lemongrass, finely chopped
Flowers from 1 stem of tuberose, petals only
½ orange, chopped into small pieces

Dressing
Pureed flesh of ½ orange
Juice of 1 limo or juice of ½ lime with a pinch of salt
1-2 tbs palm sugar
½ tsp Lao or Szechuan pepper, crushed
1 tsp good sesame oil
Sea salt to taste

Prepare all the herbs and the other ingredients and mix together just before serving. Make the dressing, adjust the seasoning to your taste and toss with the salad.
Serve immediately.

Balinese pure green *urab* vegetables with coconut

Serves 2

Ingredients

100g mixed, finely chopped vegetables & leaves of choice.
We used ferntips, Asian long green beans, winged
beans, green spinach, snowpeas & pea tendrils,
broccolini, spinach & chayote.

1 tbs crispy onions (see *Tasty Extras*)

Chop and prepare the vegetables just before serving.

Spice sauce

50g shredded coconut, fresh or dried

1 garlic clove

1 tsp turmeric

1 tsp galangal

1 tsp kencur

½ tsp coriander seed

½ tsp white peppercorns

1-2 tbs palm sugar

1 large red chilli, deseeded & chopped

1 small red chilli, deseeded & chopped

1-2 kaffir lime leaves, finely shredded

2 tbs coconut milk

1 tsp sea salt to taste

1 tbs crispy onions (see *Tasty Extras*)

Pound or grind the above together to make a paste.
Adjust the thickness of the paste and the seasoning to
your taste.

To serve

Mix the spice paste into the vegetables just before serving.
Adjust the seasoning again. Top each serving with some
crispy onions and extra sauce on the side.

Malaysian *Peranakan* red curry rice

Serves 2

Ingredients
100g oyster mushrooms, finely chopped
2 tbs galangal, minced
1 tbs garlic chives, chopped
1 tbs baby leeks, minced
50g carrots, minced
50g yam or jicama, minced
1 large red chilli, deseeded & chopped
2 cherry tomatoes, chopped

Peranakan red curry sauce
2 ripe tomatoes, chopped
2 sundried tomatoes, chopped
2 large red chillies, chopped
2 small red chillies, chopped
1 lime leaf, shredded
2 medium garlic cloves
3 shallots, minced
1 tsp tamarind pulp
½ tsp cumin powder
½ tsp fresh white peppercorns
½ tsp coriander seed
Pinch star aniseed powder
Pinch cinnamon powder
3 tbs coconut milk

Grind or blend the above together except for the coconut milk.

To serve
Just before serving, combine the 'rice' with the coconut milk, curry sauce and serve immediately.

Rawfully Good / COMO Shambhala Estate

Black rice sorbet

Serves 2

Ingredients
400g fresh young coconut
400 mls spring water
2 vanilla beans
2 tbs raw honey
100g black rice
1 tsp lime juice

Soak the black rice for 12 hours then drain well and dry before blending into a coarse powder. Blend the coconut and the water, strain well, add the black rice powder and the other ingredients. Put in an ice cream machine and process according to the manufacturer's instructions.

Spinach, cashew & coconut *basko* balls with peanut sauce & lemongrass *sambal*

Serves 2

Ingredients
100g red & green spinach, chopped
100g cashew, soaked overnight
   & well drained
100g young coconut
50g carrots, grated
2 garlic cloves
1 tbs ginger, chopped
1 small red chilli, deseeded & chopped
½ tsp coriander seeds
Pinch of fresh nutmeg
Sea salt to taste
50g Chinese celery, shredded

Prepare the above ingredients. Pound or blend into a thick paste. Leave in the fridge for 1 hour so that the flavours can develop. Adjust the seasoning before serving.

Peanut sauce
See page 26

Lemongrass *sambal*
See page 37

To serve
Wet your hands, make balls out of the cashew paste and roll in the shredded Chinese celery leaves. Put a tablespoon of peanut sauce on each plate, top with a cashew and coconut ball and serve immediately.

Vietnamese daikon parcels

Serves 2

Ingredients
1 large daikon radish, peeled & sliced lengthwise
   into paperthin slices
100g fresh peas
1 tbs Vietnamese mint or *laksa* leaf
100g fresh shitake mushrooms
1 tsp shallots, chopped
1 tsp coriander roots, chopped
1 tsp coriander leaves
1 tsp onion chives, chopped
½ tsp freshly ground black pepper
1 tsp sea salt or to taste

Slice the radish and put into a bowl with slightly salty water
to keep it crisp. Finely chop the remaining ingredients and
combine well. Drain the daikon strips and fill with the
pea and mushroom mixture. Roll up or make into parcels
adding the pea sprouts.

Red dressing
1 large red chilli, deseeded & sliced
1 small red chilli, deseeded & sliced
1 cherry tomato, chopped
1 garlic clove, chopped
1 tbs rice wine vinegar or juice of 1 lime
Pinch of white pepper
Sea salt to taste

Pound or blend the above together and adjust the seasoning.

To serve
Spoon the dressing onto each plate and top with the
daikon rolls. Serve immediately.

Coconut & vanilla pudding with passionfruit jelly & strawberries

Serves 2

Ingredients
¼ tsp agar powder
50 mls spring water
50 mls coconut water
½ tsp vanilla paste
20g palm sugar
2 passionfruits
2 tbs fresh strawberries, cut into cubes
1 tbs raw cocoa beans, chopped

Combine the agar powder with the spring water, coconut water, vanilla paste and the sugar. Heat together gently until the agar powder and the sugar are dissolved. Set aside 1 tsp of the mixture to make the passionfruit jelly. Put in small forms and leave in the fridge for at least an hour to set properly. The consistency of the jelly should not be too hard or too soft.

Mix 2 tbs fresh passionfruit juice (seeds strained out) with the 1 tsp of the coconut, water and agar mixture and put in the fridge to set.

To serve
Take the coconut jelly out of the forms and put on a plate. Chop the passionfruit jelly into small cubes, combine with the strawberry cubes and sprinkle with raw cocoa beans.

Bali

Hotel Tugu Bali, Canggu

S ituated on a quiet stretch of beach north of Seminyak, the famous party, fine dining and shopping hub of South Bali, Tugu hotel's founder Anhar Setjadibrata was able to realize one of his many dreams. This was to build a resort that would become a home to some of the many hundreds of antiques and architectural artifacts that he had collected from all over Indonesia over the years. Tugu Bali opened in 1997 very close to the place where he had bought his first antique and now one of the most prized possessions in his collection from a local priest – a 16th century stone cup for dispensing ceremonial holy water, back in his student days.

His mission has always been to design resorts that are not just luxury hotels offering every comfort, but these should also function as living museums dedicated to preserving the cultural heritage, art and handicrafts to be found in Indonesia.

Anhar not only focused on offering guests an insight into the cultural and architectural history of Java, Bali and the development of Perankan Chinese-Indonesian culture since earlier times, but aims to give his guests a comprehensive choice of very special dining experiences and extensive local menus at all his resorts so that they can sample Indonesian cuisine from all over the archipelago.

In the simple wooden Warung restaurant at Tugu Bali, all the recipes and cooking utensils used for cookery classes are purely traditional. Guests can learn how to make and experience the way in which food is prepared and served in the villages to this day. Even though Tugu's Indonesian lady chef Ibu Soelastri has cooked for Indonesian presidents, she still uses terracotta stoves and bamboo baskets for steaming rice and all her dishes are served on hand-woven coconut plates lined with freshly cut banana leaves. The ingredients she uses may appear to be refreshingly simple but the resulting tastes are complex with many different layers of interesting flavours.

Staying at any one of the many Tugu beach or city hotels is an unusual and unique cultural and culinary experience not to be missed.

Contact: Hotel Tugu Bali, Canggu Beach, Bali
Telephone: +62 361 731701 Fax: +62 362 731704
Email: bali@tuguhotels.com Web: www.tuguhotels.com

Karedok: Javanese vegetable salad with peanut sauce

Serves 2

This is a traditional Javanese salad, always made with raw vegetables. Use any kind of vegetables, but make sure that there are lots of different colours and textures.

Ingredients
100g firm tofu, cut into cubes
½ small cabbage, thinly sliced
2 small round aubergines
50g soya bean sprouts
½ cucumber, peeled, deseeded & cubed
½ small cauliflower, cut into florets
20g lemon basil leaves or sweet Thai basil leaves

Slice the aubergines thinly, then sprinkle them with salt and leave for 20 minutes then rinse and pat dry.
Cut the tofu into small cubes and the cabbage, cauliflower and cucumber into bite size pieces.

Peanut & lime sauce
100g raw peanuts, with skins if possible
2 garlic cloves, chopped
1 large and 1 small red chilli, deseeded & chopped
1 tsp tamarind paste
Juice of ½ limo or ½ lime with an extra pinch of salt
2 kaffir lime leaves, shredded
1 tbs palm sugar
1 tsp kencur, chopped
1 tsp sea salt
100 mls spring water

Pound or blend the ingredients together, adding more sugar, salt or chilli as you like.

To serve

Make the peanut sauce, adjusting the flavours and seasoning to your taste and add enough water to make a smooth dressing. Spoon some of the dressing over the salad and mix well, adding the lemon basil leaves just before serving. Put a bowl of extra dressing on the side.

Indonesian *lalapan* vegetables

Serves 2

This traditional assortment of vegetables is usually served
as a salad accompaniment. Cut vegetables of your choice
into sticks or florets and serve with the spicy sauce as a dip.

Ingredients
2 large tomatoes, cut into quarters
½ small cabbage, cut into bite size pieces
1 small cucumber, sliced
8 long beans, cut into 10 cm pieces
20g lemon basil

Sambal dipping sauce
3 large red chillies, deseeded & chopped
3 small red chillies, chopped
½ large tomato, chopped
1 tbs palm sugar
1 tsp sea salt
Juice ½ limo or juice of 1 lime mixed with a pinch of salt
1 tbs gingerflower or stem, chopped (optional)

Pound or blend the ingredients together, adjusting the
seasoning (and the amount of chillies!) to your taste.

To serve
Prepare the vegetables and arrange on a serving platter,
with the sambal dipping sauce on the side.

Balinese *lawar* with *base gde* spices

Serves 2

Ingredients
20g each red & green spinach
Juice of 1 limo or lime mixed with a pinch of salt
3 kaffir lime leaves, shredded
¼ coconut or 100g dried coconut
1 carrot, grated
¼ small cabbage, shredded
50g soy bean sprouts
200g long beans or green beans, cut very finely
50g spicy coconut (see *Tasty Extras*)
50g crispy onions (see *Tasty Extras*)
Add the vegetables and lime leaves together and just
before serving, add the coconut and spice mixture.

Base gde spice paste
2 shallots, chopped
1 stem lemongrass, outer dry part removed, finely chopped
1 small red chilli, chopped
2 garlic cloves
1 tsp coriander seeds
1 tsp black peppercorns
1 tbs turmeric, chopped
2 tbs galangal, chopped
1 tsp ginger, chopped
1 tsp kencur, chopped
1 tsp white pepper, ground
2 cm jangu (optional if not available)
Pound or grind the ingredients together well and adjust
the seasoning.

To serve
Serve each portion topped with the crispy onions and
spicy coconut.

Base or *bumbu* spice mixtures are the essence of Balinese cuisine. Every household uses their own recipes passed down through generations. These combinations of locally grown ingredients give Balinese dishes their distinctive, subtle flavours. There are two main spice mixtures, the everyday *base genep* and this special *base gde* which is prepared in staggering amounts by village men and used in the preparation of dishes served at the many village and family ceremonies. *Lawar*, a dish traditionally made with pork and long beans, is always served at Galungan or Balinese New Year festivals.

Bali

Loitering Within Tent, Ubud

D utch designer Anneke van Wasberghe created Esprite Nomade to provide a little colonial-style luxury for those who enjoy loitering within luxury tents in the Balinese countryside. She offers a full interior design service, manufactures luxury travel articles and hand-made tents of different sizes, custom made to order. Her office is situated just outside Ubud and the showroom a luxury tent in her front garden. These beautifully designed tents, filled with decorative and useful accessories that conjure up the atmosphere of colonial times gone by, are an ideal place to enjoy a 'Rawfully Good' picnic.

Recently Anneke contracted a piece of hillside land with stunning views so that she could create a more permanent place to pitch one of her Caravanserai tents, host special luxury picnics and promote the idea to possible clients all over the world.

I approached Anneke and asked her if she would let me serve a picnic as a healthy alternative menu for her Royal High Tea on the edge of the world! Usually her guests take a short walk to her secret location with spectacular views, have a soothing flower footbath on arrival, then plant a tree before enjoying a picnic served out of rattan baskets with a bottle of champagne as an optional extra for those who really want to have a picnic in style!

Just before the sun goes down, guests can do sunset yoga overlooking the gorge or have a special full-body Balinese massage in a separate massage tent serenaded only by the sounds of tropical nature settling down for the night. Afterwards they can enjoy a local, freshly-made, 'rawfully good' picnic, with a glass of champagne, of course!

Contact: Anneke van Wasberghe, Ubud, Bali, Indonesia
Telephone: +62 361 780 1847 Fax: +62 361 976630
Email: esp2000@indo.net.id Web: www.caravanseraibali.com

Rawfully Good / Loitering Within Tent

Rawfully Good / Loitering Within Tent

'Living' Asian picnic

Stuffed mushrooms with Asian salad & sesame sauce

Serves 2

Ingredients

3 or more same sized button or shitake mushrooms
    per person
4 cherry tomatoes, chopped
1 large red chilli, deseeded & chopped
1 stem lemongrass, outer leaves removed, finely sliced
2 coriander roots, finely chopped
1 tsp mint leaves, shredded
2 shallots, finely chopped
1 tbs chives, chopped

Sesame sauce

2 tbs sesame seeds
2 tbs coconut milk
1 garlic clove
Pinch fresh nutmeg
½ tsp sea salt
Spring water

Pound or blend the ingredients together, perhaps adding
some spring water to thin the dressing. Prepare all the salad
ingredients, carefully mix in the sesame sauce and stuff
the mushrooms just before serving.

Cucumber & peanut relish

Serves 2

Ingredients

2 small cucumbers, skin peeled in strips to leave a pattern,
   halved lengthways, seeds removed & sliced
100g raw peanuts, skin left on or taken off as preferred
2 shallots, finely sliced
1 bunch fresh coriander, leaves only

Dressing

150 mls white Asian vinegar
1 tbs coriander roots, chopped
2 tbs palm sugar
1 garlic clove, finely chopped
1 tbs lime juice
½ tsp sea salt or to taste
2 tbs raw sweet chilli sauce (see *Tasty Extras*)

Make the dressing and adjust the seasoning to your taste.
Sprinkle the cucumber slices with salt. Leave for 15 minutes,
then drain and pat dry. Prepare the other ingredients and
add to the cucumber slices with the dressing just before
serving. Keep cool in an airtight container.

Tempe manis

Serves 2

Ingredients
200g fresh tempeh, cut into matchsticks

Spice paste
2 garlic cloves
2 large red chilli, deseeded & finely chopped
2 tsp coriander seed
2 tbs palm sugar
1-2 tbs kecap manis or sweet soya sauce
2 tsp salt or to taste

Blend or pound all the spice paste ingredients to make a
thick paste. Adjust the seasoning before mixing it carefully
and thoroughly into the tempeh. Put in the fridge overnight
or at least 12 hours, so that the spices can be absorbed.
Spread the sticks on teflex sheets in the dehydrator.
Leave there for 15 hours at 100 degrees or until the tempeh
is crispy. Cool before keeping in an airtight container.

Zucchini flowers stuffed with cashews & sesame seeds

Serves 2

Ingredients
3 zucchini flowers per person, stamens removed
200g chopped baby vegetables such as carrots, zuccini,
  baby corn, stink beans
50g mixed basils, coriander, mint, dill, spinach leaves
  for the sauce

Cashew Paste
2 cups plain cashew nuts, soaked overnight, rinsed and
  drained well
2 tbs lime juice
2 tbs shredded mixed Asian herbs
Sea salt & white pepper to taste

Blend the drained cashews and strain through cheesecloth.
Reserve the cashew milk. Mix the cashew pulp with
enough lemon juice and cashew milk to make a thick
paste. Add the herbs and check the seasoning again.

Gently open the baby zucchini flowers. Stuff carefully
with the cashew paste mixture and press back into shape.
Blend together the mixed leaves with the remaining
cashew milk to make a dressing. Season to taste and drizzle
some on each serving plate. Arrange the zucchini flowers,
salad leaves or baby vegetables on top of the dressing
before serving.

Bali

The Chedi Club at Tanah Gajah, Ubud

Hendra Hadiprana originally built Tanah Gajah (translated as 'Land of the Elephants' because Goa Gajah, the famous 8th century Ganesha Temple is within walking distance) in 1978 as a peaceful sanctuary where his family could escape from hectic life in urban Jakarta, for entertaining his many friends from all over the world and to house his large and unique collection of modern Indonesian art. The gardens, surrounded on all sides by rice paddies, were carefully landscaped to include lakes and pools fed by streams from the rice paddies. Many different kinds of rare indigenous flora were planted, large aviaries and bird cages were built all over the property to create a home for colourful birds from all over the Archipelago.

Even though Tanah Gajah was rebuilt and opened as an hotel in 2005, the two very different worlds at Tanah Gajah – peaceful Javanese gentility and GHM Hotels stylish minimalism – exist side by side in total harmony. Some of the villas have bamboo gates that open directly into the paddy fields and even have a gas coal fire to take away the chill on damp rainy-season evenings.

These days, too, complimentary afternoon tea is served to guests in the Bird Lounge, accompanied by the sound of the whistling, singing birds in the huge aviary nearby. The carefully-tended gardens have matured beautifully and the restaurant pavilion seems to float above the surrounding paddy fields. Fireflies dance around the open windows and at night flickering candles in huge bronze candleholders add to the magic. International and both Javanese and Balinese dishes are served, using herbs and vegetables from the organic garden near the kitchen.

Hendra Hadiprana's son Sindhu watches carefully over Tanah Gajah and visits regularly. He can often be seen pottering around in the gardens or enjoying an early dinner at the restaurant.

Echoes of fond memories of lazy family days and the gentle spirits of the ricefields remain, now only the guests have changed.

Contact: The Chedi Club at Tanah Gajah, Jl. Goa Gajah, Tenglulak Kaja, Ubud, Bali 80571
Telephone: +62 361 975685 Fax: +62 361 975686
Email: chediclububud@ghmhotels.com Web: www.ghmhotels.com

Strawberry & lemon basil tarts

Makes 8 tarts

Ingredients
100g palm sugar
50g cashews (soaked overnight)
10 fresh cocoa beans
50g rice flour
Pinch sea salt

Grate the palm sugar, drain cashews well. Crush 50g
together with the cocoa beans. Add the rice flour and a
pinch of sea salt to make a thick dough. Form into small
tartlets and dehydrate for 12 hours or until crispy turning
over once.

Cashew cream
Blend 50g cashews (soaked overnight) with ¼ tsp
chopped fresh vanilla bean.

Strawberry topping
100g fresh strawberries
1 tbs chopped lemon basil
Pinch freshly ground black pepper

Chop the strawberries, add the lemon basil and a pinch
of black pepper. Spoon a layer of the cashew and vanilla
cream into the tarts and top with the strawberries.
Serve immediately at room temperature before the tarts
soften.

Bali chocolate biscuit cake

Makes 8 biscuits

Ingredients
100g cashews (soaked overnight), rinsed and drained
2 tbs vanilla bean, chopped
3 tbs rice flour
2 tbs living cocoa powder
10 cocoa beans, crushed
Pinch of sea salt

Rinse, drain and dry the cashews. Blend together with
the other ingredients and check the sweetness.
Spread on Teflex sheets (about 1 cm thick) and dehydrate
for 6 hours before turning over, cutting carefully into
rounds and dehydrating again for another 6 hours.

Filling
50g 'raw' cocoa butter
2-3 tbs virgin coconut oil
4 tbs living cocoa powder
100g palm sugar

Blend all the above ingredients together and check the
sweetness. Keep refrigerated until needed. Fill the biscuits
with the chocolate mixture and serve immediately.

Rawfully Good nut & herb Asian cracker sandwiches

Makes 8 crackers

Ingredients

Crackers
1½ cups of carrot pulp (left over from juicing)
2 small garlic cloves
50g sunflower seeds (soaked for 3 hours)
50g sesame seeds (soaked for 3 hours)
50g raw peanuts (soaked overnight)
2 ripe tomatoes, chopped
1lg red chilli, deseeded & chopped
3 tbs Thai basil, chopped
½ tsp fresh black pepper
Sea salt to taste

Drain the seeds and dry well. Finely chop the peanuts and sunflower seeds and add the sesame seeds. Blend the garlic cloves, tomatoes and carrot pulp together, add the Thai basil, chilli, fresh black pepper and sea salt to taste.

Spread the mixture on Teflex sheets (about ½ cm thick) and dehydrate for 12 hours before cutting carefully into squares, turning over and dehydrating again for 6 hours or until dry and crispy.

Sandwich filling

100g cashews (soaked overnight)
1 tbs spring onions, chopped
Inner stem of 1 lemongrass, chopped
2 small red onions, chopped
1 tomato, chopped
½ large red chilli, deseeded & chopped
2 tbs coriander leaves, chopped
1 tsp mint leaves, chopped
1 tsp dill, chopped
1 small limeleaf, shredded
Sea salt and fresh white pepper to taste

Rinse and drain the cashews well. Blend together with
the other ingredients and adjust the seasoning, adding
some spring water if the filling is too thick.

Cacao truffles
with Asian flavours

Makes approx 8 truffles

Ingredients
50g dried unsweetened coconut
3 tbs living cocoa powder
1 tbs vanilla bean, very finely chopped
2-3 tbs virgin coconut oil

Mix all the above together well, adding chopped dried fruit or nuts if you like.

Form into 2-3 cm diameter balls and refrigerate until needed in an airtight container.

Just before serving, roll the balls carefully in a coating of your choice and serve immediately.

Coatings
There are so many different coatings that you can make, according to your taste. Here we used spicy nuts (see *Tasty Extras*) with dried red chilli, green tea powder with chopped fresh mint leaves and crushed coriander seeds mixed with dried local flowers.

Bali

Alila Villas, Uluwatu

Alila's group of hotels throughout Asia is refreshingly different. Each of the properties has clean, clear-cut lines and even though the rooms or villas have very little decoration, the attention to detail is quite amazing. Alila Villas Uluwatu is the flagship for the group's new 'villa only' properties and although the resort can accommodate quite a large number of people at any given time, the atmosphere is always peaceful and the many staff quiet and attentive.

A stately entrance door made from recycled wood leads into a sitting-cum-bedroom that can be opened up from both sides allowing breezes from the Indian Ocean to cool the rooms. These private villas are tastefully decorated in soothing beige and brown tones with the large blue-tiled swimming pool adding a splash of colour. The resort cares for the environment in many ways, even the efficient, low-capacity air conditioning is the quietest ever!

Dutch Chef Stefan Zijta has worked at several Michelin star restaurants. Star-studded he may be, but he has cleverly managed to adapt his menus to complement the breezy but rather formal design of his Ciré restaurant. Overlooking the Indian Ocean far below, dining there is 'fine' at all times and even the breakfast menu served there is unique. Many daily-changing 'tasting' portions from Southeast Asia together with Western favourites, healthy or not so healthy are on offer, enabling guests who prefer to eat well in the morning to pick, choose and experiment with different tastes and flavours.

Stefan also oversees The Warung, a cool restaurant that serves purely Balinese and Indonesian cuisine, family-style at a nine meter long wooden table or at quiet tables on the terrace outside. This is where we prepared the 'rawfully good' lunch menu together by adapting some traditional Dutch-Indonesian recipes. Stephan and I are already planning a series of 'Rawfully Good Days' of 'living' cooking classes followed by gourmet dinners paired with specially chosen vegan wines.

The property is an ideal sanctuary to relax, and, although many interesting activities and excursions are available, because the property is situated on the very southern tip of Bali, it may be better just stay in the resort, enjoy the food, have some spa treatments and take a well-earned rest. A peaceful day doing nothing at all followed by a prolonged afternoon nap on the huge day bed could culminate with rolling over into the private pool.

Contact: Alila Villas Uluwatu, Jalan Belimbing Sari, Banjar Tambiyak
Desa Pecatu, Bali, Indonesia. Telephone: +62 361 848 2166 Fax: +62 361 848 2277
Email: uluwatu@alilahotels.com Web: www.alilahotels.com

'Living' red bean soup

Serves 2

Ingredients
100g tiny red adzuki beans
   (soaked overnight then sprouted for 3 days)
1 tsp fresh ginger, minced
½ garlic clove, minced
½ tsp kencur, minced
½ inside stem of lemongrass, finely chopped
¼ tsp vegan stock powder
¼ tsp palm sugar or to taste
Juice of ½ lime
1 small lime leaf, shredded
Sea salt to taste
Tiny lemon basil leaves and minced red chilli for decoration.

Purée the beans, leaving some to garnish the soup, together
with the other ingredients, adding a tablespoon or two of
either spring or fresh coconut water if the soup is too thick.
Put in the fridge for an hour or two so that the flavours can
develop. Adjust the seasoning before serving and garnish
with the beans, leaves and minced chilli.

'Living' Asian lunch

Serves 6

Peanut rissoles on cucumber salad

100g raw, shelled peanuts (soaked overnight)
100g block tofu, drained
1 tsp Chinese celery leaf, chopped
½ tsp coriander seed, crushed
1 tbs spring onions, chopped
1 tsp red onions, minced
½ tsp fresh white pepper
Sea salt to taste.
Rinse and drain the peanuts well. Blend with the tofu to make a
thick cream. Add all the other ingredients and mix well.
Put the cream aside for an hour so that all the flavours can
develop. Before serving, check and adjust the seasoning again.

Cucumber salad

1 young Lebanese or Asian cucumber, peeled in stripes
    lengthways and cut into matchstick pieces
Juice ½ lime
½ tsp red onion, chopped
½ tsp palm sugar or to taste
Salt to taste
Make the dressing and add the cucumber sticks.
Marinade for 15 minutes before serving.

To serve

Using two tablespoons or an ice cream scoop, form portions of
the cream and place on top of the cucumber salad.

Black Sesame *sambal*

2 tbs black sesame seeds
 (soaked overnight & drained)
½ tsp white peppercorns, crushed
1 tbs fresh coconut or spring water
1 tsp coriander seeds, crushed
5 tbs cashews (soaked overnight, rinsed & drained)
Palm sugar to taste
Juice ½ lime
Sea salt to taste
Blend or pound all the above ingredients together and adjust
the seasoning before serving.

'Living' Young corn crackers (Serves 8-10)

4 young corn cobs, scraped
1 tsp kencur, chopped
½ large chilli, deseeded & chopped
3 red onions, chopped
1 garlic clove, chopped
1 tsp Chinese celery leaves, finely chopped
Sea salt to taste
Pound all the above ingredients together in a mortar and
adjust the seasoning to your taste. Wet your hands and
carefully form rounds out of the mixture. Place on Teflex
sheets and dehydrate for 12 hours on one side. Turn over and
dehydrate again until firm.

'Living' Asian lunch

Balinese young papaya salad with crunchy river sprinkle (Serves 2)
100g green, young papaya, coarsely grated
100g young coconut meat, cut into thin slivers or
4 tbs dried coconut, soaked in 2 tbs spring water
4 baby tomatoes, thinly sliced lengthways
1 tbs black rice, soaked for 24 hours & drained well

Spice paste
2 tsp virgin coconut oil
1 tsp fresh turmeric, chopped
1 small red chilli, chopped
1 garlic clove, chopped
2 red onions, chopped
½ tsp coriander seed
½ tsp tamarind paste
½ tsp fresh black peppercorns
Palm sugar to taste
2 baby tomatoes, chopped
Sea salt to taste

Blend or pound the above together and adjust the seasoning to your taste. Set aside so that the flavours can develop.

Just before serving, mix the young papaya, coconut and tomatoes together, adding the spice paste little by little. Mix carefully and if you have added too much spice paste by mistake, add some coconut milk or coconut water. Sprinkle with the crunchy black rice and serve immediately.

Rawfully Good / Alila Uluwatu Villas

No sugar Asian delight

Serves 2

Ingredients
200g fresh, young coconut meat
100g cashews (soaked overnight)
Juice ½ lime
¼ tsp finely chopped fresh vanilla bean
Pinch sea salt
Freshly grated nutmeg

Cut half of the young coconut meat into pieces and set aside. Rinse and drain the cashews and blend together with the other half of the coconut meat, lime juice, vanilla bean and sea salt.

Add the remaining coconut and mix carefully.
Put into individual serving bowls, grate some fresh nutmeg over the top and put in the fridge for an hour before serving.

Thailand

Chakrabongse Villas, Bangkok

When Narisa Chakrabongse – a member of Thailand's royal family who successfully changed her father's beautiful villa on the Chao Phraya river in old Bangkok into a small hotel in 2004 – came to Puri Ganesha in 2008, we both had no idea just how interested she and her family would be not only to try my 'rawfully good' food but spend days enjoying it.

Narisa grew up in two very different worlds, enjoying a laid-back country life in Cornwall, England, and contrasting rather formal and traditional life of royalty in Old Bangkok. The common thread in both places was always being able to enjoy the most delicious food. Vegetables for the English food at home in Cornwall came from their huge vegetable garden. Fresh fruit was grown in special cages, hot houses and an orchard. In Bangkok, Mae Prayong the cook, who had been with the family for 30 years, concocted marvellous recipes with completely different Thai flavours: coconut, lime, lemongrass, coriander, ripe and unripe mango and papaya and, when she was old enough, chillis. As a child, she loved to go to the kitchen and watch the cook pounding spices in a large granite mortar, seated on an enormous, low wooden table.

Accordingly, when Narisa opened her Bangkok home as an hotel, she was determined that her guests should be able to experience the vey best authentic but light and healthy Thai cuisine. She began to grow her own herbs and spices and because Chakrabongse Villas is close to the best fruit and vegetable market in Bangkok, buying the freshest possible produce for her kitchens was easy.

Narisa was already a proto-vegetarian and when she came to Puri Ganesha she discovered how to give vegetarian food exquisite new tastes, textures, colours and a particularly vibrant 'zing'. A far cry from the heavy, predominantly brown colours and bland tastes of vegetarian food still to be found on many restaurant menus since the 1970s, she found the raw food flavours and presentation at Puri Ganesha to be more like those at home in Thailand.

When I was working on recipes at Chakrabongse Villas with chef Vat, I was happy to find that my style of food immediately struck an harmonious chord with all the kitchen staff, even though I flatly refused to use any animal products at all. To begin with, no one in the kitchen believed that I could produce anything remotely edible without using the ubiquitous *nam pla* fish sauce at all!

Narisa's peaceful Chakrabongse Villas is situated in the most historic area of Bangkok, where there are so many exciting things to discover. Far away from the mundane shopping malls of Sukhumvit, the slower pace of life in the palace and temple district of Tatien is steeped in tradition. Stay in one of the beautiful suites, get up early to follow the monks on their morning alms' round, then have breakfast overlooking the busy river. Explore the famous local temples and palaces with a guide by bicycle or enjoy a river cruise on the villa's private launch. Relax with a Thai-style massage in the afternoon before feasting on wonderfully fresh Thai food in the colourful pavilion by the river. The staff are happy to suggest interesting outings and boat trips to some of the famous local restaurants nearby.

Just before Narisa, who also owns River Books, a specialized publisher of beautiful books on the art, archaeology and cultures of Mainland Southeast Asia, left Puri Ganesha, she asked me if I would like to write their very first cookbook and *Rawfully Good* is the result.

Contact: Chakrabongse Villas, 396 Maharaj Rd, Tatien, Bangkok 10200, Thailand
Telephone: +66 (0) 2222 1290 Fax: +66 (0) 2225 3861
Email: reservation@thaivillas.com Web: www.thaivillas.com

Spicy Thai fruit salad

Serves 2

Ingredients
3 tbs green papaya, shredded
½ pomelo or grapefruit flesh
½ pineapple, chopped into bite size pieces
3 tbs mango, chopped
4 strawberries, chopped
2 shallots, finely sliced
1 tbs ginger, finely chopped

Dressing
1 small red & 1 small green chilli, deseeded & chopped
1 tsp tamarind paste mixed with a little water
2 tbs palm sugar or more to taste
Sea salt to taste

Chop or shred the fruit and put in a bowl.
Make the dressing and adjust the seasoning.
Serve immediately topped with edible flowers or herbs.

Young green fruit salad with sweet chilli dressing

Serves 4

Ingredients
100g young papaya, grated
100g young mango, grated
50g carrots, grated
2 inside stems lemongrass, finely sliced
20g soya beansprouts
20g fresh galangal, grated
20g fresh ginger, grated
4 shallots, finely sliced
1 medium kaffir lime leaf, shredded
2 large mint leaves, shredded

Prepare the ingredients for the salad, mix together
and set aside.

Dressing
5 tbs sweet chilli sauce (see *Tasty Extras*)
2 tbs lime juice
Salt to taste
Chopped chilli & coriander leaves to garnish
1 tbs spicy nuts (see *Tasty Extras*)

To serve
Either mix the dressing with the salad just before serving
or put the dressing in a separate bowl. Garnish with
more chilli and coriander leaves, herbs of your choice
and spicy peanuts.

Thai green curry

Serves 2

Ingredients
12 Thai pea aubergines
2-3 baby aubergines, finely sliced and soaked in salty water
    for 30 mins to remove any bitter taste. Pat dry before use
100 fresh shitake or other mushrooms
2 heads of broccoli, finely chopped
2 tbs sliced snow peas
2 tbs coriander leaves, roughly chopped

Green curry paste
6 tbs coconut milk
4 shallots, chopped
1 garlic clove, chopped
1 tbs galangal, chopped
1 cm ginger, chopped
1 tbs green chillies, deseeded & chopped
1 tbs inner lemongrass stem, finely sliced
1 tbs Thai holy basil leaves
1 tbs Thai sweet basil leaves
1 tbs coriander roots, chopped
2 kaffir lime leaves, finely shredded
1-2 tbs palm sugar or to taste
1 tsp green peppercorns, crushed
Juice of 1-2 limes
Sea salt to taste

Pound or grind all the green curry paste ingredients together.
Add the coconut milk and thin to the desired consistency
with spring or coconut water before adding the spices,
herbs and vegetables. Warm through gently and garnish
with more herbs and chillies.

To serve
Serve with finely chopped cauliflower 'rice', cooked natural
brown or red rice.

A 'living' version of traditional *mieng kam*

Serves 2

Ingredients
5 pieces of wild betel or pepper leaves (alternatively, use
    spinach, cabbage or any crisp lettuce leaves cut into the
    same size pieces) per person
100g fresh coconut cut into tiny cubes or use dried,
    shredded (but unsweetened) coconut
50g galangal & 50g ginger, peeled & cut into tiny cubes
2 thin-skinned limes, seeds taken out & chopped into
    tiny triangles
50g small green and red chillies, deseeded & very finely
    chopped
50g raw or spicy raw peanuts (see *Tasty Extras*)
4 shallots, finely sliced
2 tbs coriander leaves

Dipping sauce
20g galangal, chopped
20g ginger, chopped
2 small shallots, chopped
1 large clove of garlic
2 tbs palm sugar
1 tbs thick honey
Sea salt to taste

Thais have many variations for this popular snack and
usually serve it in one of two different ways. One way is
to chop all the ingredients very finely and then make into
beautifully artistic little rolls or triangles. The second,
much easier and less time-consuming way is to heap
small piles of the ingredients around the leaves to be used
or put them into separate little bowls, so that everyone
can choose whatever they like to make their own.

Thai glass noodles with asparagus & green pepper dressing

Serves 2

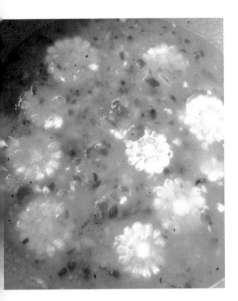

Ingredients

250g very fine rice noodles
2 baby round aubergines, sliced &
    soaked in water with a pinch of salt
    for 30 mins to remove the bitter taste
6 stems green asparagus, sliced
1 tbs galangal, chopped
2 tbs white cabbage, shredded
1 tbs Chinese celery leaves, chopped
1 large kaffir lime leaf, finely shredded

Soak the rice noodles in warm water
with a pinch of salt until soft.
Drain and set aside.

Green pepper dressing

1 tsp green peppercorns
4 tbs coconut milk
2 shallots, chopped
1 garlic clove, chopped
1 tbs palm sugar
Juice of ½ -1 lime
1 kaffir lime leaf, shredded
1 baby sweetcorn, sliced (optional)

Finely chop the green peppercorns, add the other
ingredients to make a dressing and set aside.
Prepare the green pepper dressing first and set aside.
Chop the vegetables and just before serving, mix into the
drained noodles. Garnish with herbs or edible flowers of
choice.

Spice up your life

Serves 2

Ingredients
2 small cucumbers, deseeded & chopped
4 shallots, chopped
2 tbs large red chillies, finely sliced
3 tbs white vinegar
3 tbs palm sugar
Sea salt to taste

This little side salad is the Thai version of Indonesian
acar. It is usually served at every meal to give an added
'crunch' to coconut milk curries and it will keep in the
fridge overnight. Chop the cucumbers, shallots and
chillies. Make a dressing with the vinegar, palm sugar and
salt and adjust the flavours before adding to the other
ingredients.

Vegetable *laab*

Serves 2

Ingredients
2 tbs carrots, shredded
4 shallots, finely sliced
2 tbs cucumber, chopped
4 long green beans, finely sliced
1 large green chilli, deseeded & chopped
2 stems kalian, or green cabbage, with
    yellow or white flowers, chopped
2 heads of broccoli
4 cherry tomatoes, chopped
6 pieces sawtooth coriander, shredded or
2 tbs coriander leaves
2 tbs sweet & holy Thai basil leaves,
    roughly chopped
2 kaffir lime leaves, finely shredded
2 tsp chives, chopped

Dressing
4 mint leaves, shredded
2 small green chillies, chopped
3 tbs palm sugar
2 tbs lime juice
Sea salt to taste

Chop or shred all the ingredients as finely as possible and
mix with the dressing just before serving.
Serve at room temperature.
Garnish with edible flowers or herbs.

Three fruit slice with vanilla & coconut sauce

Serves 2

For this recipe, any available fruits can be used but make sure that they have contrasting tastes and colours.

Ingredients
¼ ripe watermelon
½ ripe honeydew melon
½ ripe green melon or slices of any kind of three different
fruits of choice

Cut the fruit into 3 equal-sized squares or rectangles for each portion then make different 'sandwiches' mixing the fruits and colours. Decorate with three different chopped fruits, edible flower or sorbet toppings.

Sauce
½ tsp pure vanilla paste
4 tbs coconut milk
2 mint leaves, finely chopped
Lime juice to taste

Blend the above together well. Adjust the flavours of the sauce as you prefer.

To serve
Cover two plates with the sauce before arranging the fruit slices on top. Add the toppings just before serving.

Thailand

Mekong Villas, Ban Huai Faen, Loei province

Upon arrival at Narisa's magical, rural retreat in the beautiful, unspoile northeastern province of Loei, the long eight-hour drive from Bangok soon forgotten. Her wooden villas, built on different levels in Norther Thai style overlook the Mekong River and Laos beyond. Loei is one of the few onl provinces in Thailand where temperatures can dip to below zero in December s remember to pack socks and sweaters!

This is a secluded, peacefu hideaway for guests who jus like to enjoy spectacula scenery, perhaps trek in th region's famous national park or visit nearby Chiang Khan, picturesque, historical villag with wooden shop houses o the bank of the Mekong wher time seems to have stood sti for years.

Northeastern Thai foo shares the same basic culinar heritage as neighbouring Lac with edible flowers and fres herbs playing an essential rol in both cuisines. On the Thai side of the Mekong River every eating place, no matte how small, places rows of brightly coloured plastic buckets filled with fresh herbs o each table. An interesting part of the culinary landscape is to see all the different herb growing outside each house in plant pots made out of recycled rubber car tyres.

Many of the ingredients for the following recipes were found in Narisa's natura garden, but what a treat it was to find so many edible flowers, interesting herbs an unusual vegetables at the local morning market.

Back at the villas, the dressings were prepared first and set aside at room temperature so that the flavours could develop. Just before serving all the ingredient were cleaned, chopped and the dressings were added. The food tasted even better b candlelight under a full moon over the Mekong River!

Contact: Mekong Villas, Ban Huai Faen, 96 Moo 6, Leab Mekong Road, Ban Kok Pa Pachom District, Loei Province
Telephone: +66 (0) 2222 1290 Fax: +66 (0) 2225 3861
Email: reservation@thaivillas.com Web: www.thaivillas.com

Rawfully Good / Ban Huai Faen Mekong Villas

Wild Loei salad
with green dressing

Serves 2

Ingredients
A handful of edible flower petals
A handful of oriental or mixed herbs, leaves only
1 tsp ginger, finely chopped
2 lime leaves, shredded
2 small red chillies, deseeded & chopped
1 tsp Chinese keys or galangal, chopped
Inside of 2 stems lemongrass, sliced

Green dressing
Juice of 1-2 limes
2 garlic cloves
1 small green chilli, deseeded & chopped
1 large green chilli, deseeded & chopped
1 tsp kaffir lime zest
1 tbs coriander root
1 tsp coriander seed
1 tsp galangal, chopped
1 tbs palm sugar or to taste
1 cm turmeric, chopped
Black pepper, crushed
Sea salt to taste
3 tbs coconut milk
1 tbs water

Blend or pound the dressing ingredients together to make
a smooth paste, adding water or lime juice to thin it down
to the consistency you like. Just before serving, adjust the
seasonings, add to the salad and toss carefully.

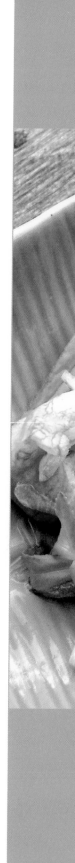

Mekong garden salad with red curry dressing

Serves 2

Ingredients
Simply take some fresh vegetables, chop or shred fresh herbs and edible flowers. Perhaps just substitute spinach, fennel, chicory, cress and cabbage, or whatever is available!

Red curry dressing
6 small dried red chillies, deseeded & soaked in warm water until soft then chopped
2 small fresh red chillies, chopped
4 shallots, chopped
2 garlic cloves, chopped
1 tbs fresh galangal, chopped
1 tsp coriander seeds
Pinch cumin seeds
Inside of two stems of lemongrass, finely sliced
2 tbs coriander root or coriander stems & leaves
2 kaffir lime leaves, shredded
Juice 1-2 limes
2 tbs palm sugar or to taste
Sea salt to taste

Pound or blend the above together and adjust the dressing to your taste. Add water or lime juice to make a dressing in case the paste is too thick. Just before serving, carefully spoon the dressing over the vegetables and herbs and mix well. Serve immediately and garnish with more herbs or edible flowers.

Northern Thai mixed mushroom salad

Serves 2

Ingredients

200g mixed mushrooms, cleaned & sprinkled with
    lime juice
50g carrots, shredded
4 shallots, finely sliced
1 tbs spring onions, chopped
1 tbs Chinese celery leaves

Dressing

1 tbs palm sugar or more to taste
2 tbs lime juice
1 small red chilli, deseeded and finely chopped
Sea salt to taste

Make the dressing first and set aside for 30 minutes so
that the flavours can develop. Meanwhile chop the
mushrooms and make the salad. Adjust the flavours of the
dressing and just before serving, add to the salad.
Serve with extra spring onions and crispy onions on top.

Winged bean salad

Serves 2

Ingredients
200g winged beans
100g carrots, shredded
4 shallots, finely sliced
1 tsp dried red chilli flakes or ½ fresh red chilli
1 tbs dried coconut
1 tbs coriander leaves
1 tbs sweet basil leaves
2 tbs spicy peanuts (see *Tasty Extras*)

Dressing
1 small red chilli, chopped
2 tbs lime juice
3 tbs palm sugar
Sea salt to taste

Grind or blend the dressing and adjust seasonings to taste.
Cut down the sides of the beans to remove any stringy
bits and slice finely. Add the other ingredients and mix
well before pouring over the dressing. Mix again and
check the flavours before serving.

Thailand

Rachamankha, Chiang Mai

C hiang Mai, the Northern capital and second largest city in Thailand, has a chequered history. It was considered to be a great prize and was much fought-over by warring neighbours for more than seven hundred years. Separated geographically from the rest of Thailand until the railway arrived in 1921, the rich Lanna ('one million ricefields') kingdom enjoyed a golden age in the 15th century. This legacy has resulted in the city having some of the most beautiful examples of Buddhist temple architecture in the country, being an interesting melting pot for hill tribe cultures with their many different cuisines and developing into a centre for the flourishing local ethnic design trade.

Food has always been an essential part of Thai culture and in the Chiang Mai region, Tai-Yai or Shan cuisine – these people migrated from Burma in the 19th century and are still one of the largest ethnic groups living in the area – plays one of the most important roles with more tangy, saltier flavours preferred over the sweetness of southern Thai cuisine. On every plate and in each bowl of northern food, the diverse ingredients pay homage to a culinary heritage borrowed from the cuisines of neighbouring China, India, Laos and Burma.

The city has a temperate climate and the cooler 'winter' season between November and February supports diverse kinds of agriculture, resulting in an enormous seasonal array of fresh indigenous produce grown in the surrounding villages being delivered to the local markets every day. Many natural 'jungle' foods such as wild herbs, plants and edible flowers replace the spicy coconut and seafood ingredients of the south.

I was lucky to be able to work with Chef Supawat at Rachamankha. Completed in 2004, this is one of the most peaceful and beautiful hotels I have ever visited. Built within the original historic city walls, and in walking distance of the city's largest temple complex Wat Phra Singh, the hotel is the ideal place to relax after undertaking temple visits, jungle or shopping tours and is possibly a place you might never want to leave! The carefully designed and executed buildings echo the simple Lanna style of temple architecture and although guests have the feeling that they could be staying in an ancient monastery, no modern convenience has been forgotten or any tiny detail overlooked. Carefully chosen artworks reflect the varied cultural history of the region and special pieces from mainland China have found a home alongside the many Thai, Lao and Burmese antiques.

The hotel menu offers a wide variety of Tai-Yai, Burmese and Lao cusines and versatile Chef Supawat gave me some very simple Tai-Yai recipes to work with. As you will see from the following recipes, they are very easy to prepare but the ingredients must be really fresh to bring out the single, intense flavours in each dish. He has since created a new 'raw' food menu for guests which we hope to be developing in the future, perhaps even adding a 'rawfully good' version of the most famous northern noodle dish khao soi!

Contact: Rachamankha, 6 Rachamankha 9, Phra Singh, Chiang Mai, 50200
Telephone: +66 53 904111 Fax: +66 53 904114
Email: sales@rachamankha.com Web: www.rachamankha.com

Northern Thai coriander salad

Serves 2

Ingredients
2 large bunches of coriander, stems & leaves chopped
2 small dried red chillies, soaked in warm water to
    rehydrate, drained & chopped
2 garlic cloves, chopped
1 tsp sesame oil
1 tbs good salad oil
Sea salt and white pepper to taste

Prepare the chillis and the other ingredients and mix
together. Adjust the seasoning before adding the coriander
leaves and stems. Serve this salad immediately after
preparing it so that the coriander leaves do not wilt.

Tofu & lemongrass salad

Serves 2

Ingredients
100g soya beansprouts or other sprouts
Inside of 3 stems of lemongrass, very finely sliced
2 spring onions, chopped
1 tsp Chinese celery leaves, chopped
1 tbs mint leaves, shredded

Dressing
1 tbs lime juice
1 tbs coconut oil
¼ tsp white pepper
Sea salt to taste
1 tbs crispy shallots and more mint leaves to garnish

Prepare the salad ingredients. Make the dressing and adjust
the seasoning. Just before serving, mix the dressing into
the salad and top with mint leaves and crispy shallots
(see *Tasty Extras*).

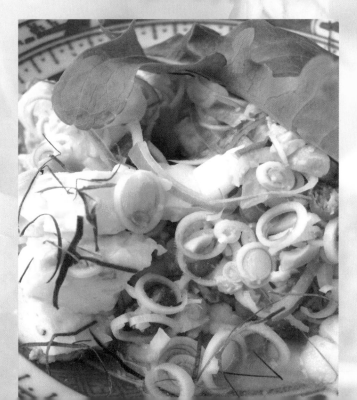

Tai Yai beansprout salad

Serves 2

Ingredients
100g soya beansprouts or other sprouts
Inside of 3 stems of lemongrass, very finely sliced
2 spring onions, chopped
1 tsp Chinese celery leaves, chopped
1 tbs mint leaves, shredded
1 tbs lime juice
1 tbs coconut oil
¼ tsp white pepper
Sea salt to taste
1 tbs crispy shallots and more mint leaves to garnish

Prepare the salad ingredients. Make the dressing and adjust
the seasoning. Just before serving, mix in the dressing and
top with mint leaves and crispy shallots (see *Tasty Extras*).

Tai Yai thick rice noodles with herbs

Serves 2

Ingredients
200g thick rice noodles
20g Thai holy basil
20g Thai sweet basil
20g thick onion chives
4 shallots, finely sliced
2 ripe tomatoes, sliced

Sauce
2 tbs tamari soy sauce
1 tsp good sesame oil
½ tsp white pepper
Sea salt to taste

Finely shred the basils. Chop the chives and garlic.
Slice the shallots. Make the sauce and adjust the seasoning.
Soak the rice noodles in hand hot water for 5 minutes until
they are soft, keep warm. Drain carefully just before
serving and adding the herbs and the sauce. Toss together
carefully so as not to break up the noodles and check the
seasoning again. Serve warm on slices of ripe tomato.
Garnish with more of the herbs.

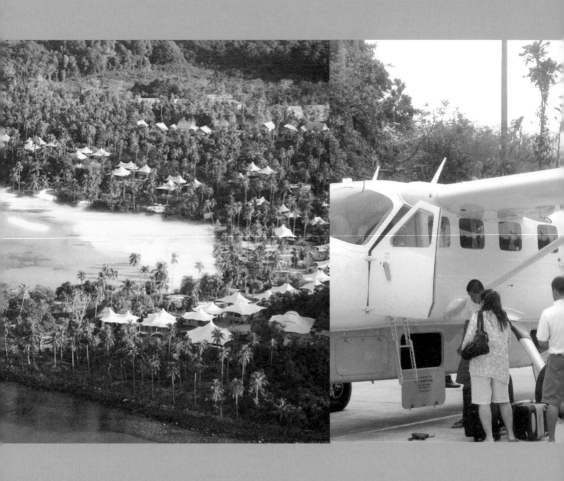

Thailand

Soneva Kiri by Six Senses, Koh Kood

Six Senses have always been pioneers in trying to recreate and rediscover the SLOW LIFE (Sustainable, Local, Organic, Wholesome, Learning, Inspiring, Fun, Experiences) and while no small detail is forgotten, barefoot luxury remains the code for any holiday at one of their resorts.

The excitement of reaching the newest Six Senses resort Soneva Kiri on Koh Kood Island begins with just over an hour's flight by private, 8-seater Cessna Caravan. This small *Ever Soneva Over the Top* plane is fitted with pale grey leather seats and affords the best possible views of Thailand's southeastern islands. Descending onto a private airstrip on the neighbouring island, guests are greeted by their own personal *Friday* butler who runs them down to the jetty for the 5 minute boat trip to the resort.

On arrival, guests walk through an artistic bamboo tunnel to discover a resort beautifully crafted from stone, recycled timber, bamboo and other natural materials. Careful attention has been paid to keeping the fragile environmental balance of the island while running a luxury property at the same time, culminating in luxurious ecological design as seen in the specially built Eco Villa.

This is a laid-back luxury resort with colonial touches, where each villa has it's own electric buggy and bicycles to cover the distances between the villas, different dining options and the spa. The Beach Villas are so spacious, it's easy to get lost at the outset. Each one has wrap-around private pools and open, tented bathrooms with washbasins set into huge cabin trunks. The bedroom doors can be folded back to let in the sounds of the jungle birds. The swimming pool is a few steps down from the most comfortable bed I have ever slept in!

Dining options are many and the main restaurant houses the signature cheese and cold cuts room, more than 50 different flavours of ice cream and a small, air-conditioned room filled with all kinds of totally wicked homemade chocolate creations.

Executive Chef Jaume Esperalba worked at the fabled El Bulli restaurant in Spain and now brings his passion for food to Soneva Kiri. *Benz's* traditional Thai seafood restaurant can only be reached by boat or dine at Chef Adam's *Sense with a View* fine dining restaurant and enjoy a daily-changing menu strongly influenced by local produce.

Apart from being able to relax in comfort, Soneva Kiri is the ideal place to relax and enjoy good, fresh food, both traditional and innovative!

Contact: Soneva Kiri by Six Senses
110 Moo 4, Koh Road, Koh Kood, Trat 23000, Thailand
Telephone: +66 (0)39 619 800 Fax: +66 (0) 39 619 808
Email: reservations-kiri@sixsenses.com Web: www.sixsenses.com

Tom yam soup
with edible Thai flowers

Serves 2

Ingredients
6 medium tomatoes, chopped
2 tbs coriander leaves & stems
1 tbs lime juice
1 lime leaf, finely shredded
½ inside stem of 1 lemongrass
½-1 tsp palm sugar or to taste
¼ tsp agar poweder
2 small red chilli, deseeded & chopped
1 tsp galangal, chopped
Pinch white pepper
Sea salt to taste

Blend all the above together. Pour into a piece of
muslin and hang over a bowl until approximately
150 ml of liquid can be measured. Add just a little
more than ¼ tsp agar powder to the liquid, stir well
until smooth and set aside for 10 minutes until just
solid enough to work with. Put two plating rings on
a silicone sheet and carefully spoon in the mixture
until it is ½ cm thick. Place in the fridge for 30
minutes. Using a wet palette knife, gently slide the
mixture onto serving plates and just before serving
decorate with edible flowers, pieces of baby vegetables
or herbs of your choice.

Jewelled green 'rice' with Asian mushroom slaw

Serves 2

Ingredients

'Rice'
200g mixed mushroom stems & cauliflower, finely chopped
3 tbs coriander leaf, lime leaf, Thai basil, small green
    chilli, spring onions or chives, all very finely chopped
Pinch freshly grated nutmeg
1 tbs coconut milk
Sea salt to taste
Black sesame seeds to garnish

Chop the above ingredients very finely to look like 'rice',
season to taste and set aside so that the flavours can develop.
Adjust seasoning again before serving.

Asian mushroom slaw
100g Asian mushrooms, rinsed quickly to remove any soil
    and pat dry carefully
200g mixed green vegetables: bok choy, Chinese cabbage,
    kale, cucumber, green mango or papaya, peeled & sliced

Slaw dressing
½ tsp coriander seeds
1 tsp palm sugar
Inside stem of 1 lemongrass, finely chopped
2 lime leaves, shredded
Juice ½-1 lime
1-2 tsp tamari sauce
½ tsp good sesame oil
Sea salt to taste

Just before serving, slice the mushrooms, mix with the
green vegetables and toss carefully with the dressing.

Sweet & sour tofu on spiced carrot & papaya puree

Serves 2

Ingredients
100g firm tofu, cut into small cubes
1 tsp chives, chopped for garnish

Tofu paste
1 small dried chilli, soak in 1 tbs water, drained & chopped
2 small red onions, minced
1 small garlic clove, minced
Inside stem of 1 lemongrass, minced
½ tsp fresh turmeric, minced
1 tsp raw peanuts, finely crushed
Raw honey to taste
Sea salt to taste

Blend or pound the above together to a paste.
Add some spring water or lime juice if the mixture is too
thick. Set aside so that the flavours can develop.

Spiced carrot & papaya puree
50g carrots, chopped
50g medium ripe papaya, chopped
2 tbs young coconut meat
½ tsp fresh ginger, chopped
½ tsp fresh galangal, chopped
½ tsp coriander seed
1 tsp lime juice
1 tsp orange juice
½ tsp white pepper
Sea salt to taste

Blend the ingredients, ensuring that the mixture is not too
runny. If it is, add more chopped carrots until the mixture
has the consistency of a thick puree. Adjust the seasoning
again. Just before serving, adjust the tofu paste seasoning to
your taste and mix it carefully with the cubed tofu.

Daikon 'noodles' with coconut dressing & vegetables

Serves 2

Ingredients
1 large daikon, peeled

Coconut dressing
1 small green and 1 small red chilli,
   deseeded & finely chopped
¼ tsp cumin seeds crushed with
½ tsp coriander seed
1 tsp galangal, chopped
1 tsp ginger, chopped
1 tbs virgin coconut oil
½ tbs chilli oil
Juice of 1 lime
1 tsp tamari
Palm sugar & sea salt to taste

Blend or pound the above together, adding more liquid
if the mixture is too thick. With a mandoline, shave the
daikon into long, wide 'noodles'. Put into a bowl of iced
water with a little salt and lime juice to crisp.

Salad garnish
Use a little of whatever you can find that has different
colours and textures: beansprouts, shredded pepper leaves,
young coconut, shredded dried coconut, chilli flakes,
green mango or papaya, green peppercorns, stink beans,
sliced shitake, fresh peas, edible flowers etc.

Just before serving, drain the 'noodles' and carefully
pat dry. Toss with the dressing, adjusting the seasoning.
Add the salad and vegetable garnish. Serve immediately.

Sapodilla & snakefruit sorbet with rose apple & pomelo

Makes approx 20 scoops of sorbet

Ingredients
1 ltr spring water
500g sapodilla fruit, peeled, stoned & chopped
500g snakefruit, peeled, stoned & chopped
3-4 tbs Mai Si (local) or any other good 'raw' honey
1 fresh vanilla bean, minced
Pinch of finely crushed star aniseed seed
Tiny pinch of sea salt

Puree all the above ingredients together and add more honey or palm sugar if preferred. Put the mixture in an ice cream maker and process according to the manufacturer's instructions.

Rose apple & pomelo salad
2 dark red rose apples
½ pomelo
Juice of 1 lime
1 tsp palm sugar or to taste

Chop and de-pip the rose apples, shred the pomelo, add lime juice & palm sugar to taste.

Peanut garnish
1 tbs peanuts, finely chopped
1 tbs palm sugar to taste, finely grated

Mix the above together well and use as a sprinkle or garnish.

Malaysia

Templetree & Bon Ton Resort, Langkawi

Australian owner, visionary and animal helper Narelle McMurtie has always had a soft spot for food and historic buildings. She ran a restaurant in Kuala Lumpur before moving to Langkawi to build her fabled Bon Ton Resort. Facing a lagoon and the sea beyond, Narelle carefully renovated the eight, up to century old wooden Malay villas to include all modern comforts without them losing any of their original antique identities.

Well-frequented as a favourite meeting place for both locals and guests from other resorts, the Nam restaurant prepares really authentic, fresh Malaysian *laksa*, curries and international dishes all day and late into the evening. A private dining room overlooking the lagoon is also available for small, intimate dinners or just for a romantic supper – all the food served here is consistently good.

Just over the wall from Bon Ton is Narelle's latest project. Not content with her eight lovely antique houses at Bon Ton, she just had to take her passion for historic buildings a step further. Together with the help of friends and investors she managed to source, transport and rebuild eight more examples of Malaysian historical architecture, each one completely different and stunning in its own way. Finished in 2009, guests can now meet in the Straits Clubhouse reception, a beautifully rebuilt 1920s house from Georgetown, Penang for meals or a drink at the bar, swim in one of the two lap pools or just enjoy discovering the different styles of architecture.

Narelle also has great plans to restore some old shop houses in the UNESCO heritage area of Georgetown in Penang. Guests staying here in the future will be able to discover the old town and enjoy trying the many different cuisines that this Asian foodlovers' paradise has to offer.

Narelle's other passion is her LASSie Foundation, www.langkawielassie.org.my, funded by donations, which saves and shelters stray cats and dogs from all over the island.

Although the markets in Langkawi are not as interesting or offer as many ingredients as those in other parts of Southeast Asia, *kerabu* salads and the *nasi ulam* dishes packed full of fresh wild and cultivated herbs and leaves, have become some of my all time favourites. Working with all the wonderful staff in the kitchens at Bon Ton, I learned how to dye my 'rice' blue using a natural dye, while wild leaves could be shredded to use in *ulams* or salads. In return, I showed them that fish paste is not an ingredient that has to be included in simply everything and that freshly prepared 'living' vegetable dishes can also taste fresh and healthy too!

Contact: Bon Ton Restaurant & Resort, Pantai Cenang, 07000 Langkawi. Malaysia
Telephone: +60 4 955 1688 Fax: + 60 4 955 4791
Email: info@bontonresort.com.my
Web: www.bontonresort.com.my and www.templetree.com.my

Galangal salad

Serves 2

Ingredients

10 cm galangal, peeled & chopped
100g freshly grated coconut or
50g dessicated coconut chopped
1 large green and 1 large red chilli, deseeded
  & finely chopped
2 stalks lemongrass, outer leaves removed,
  inner part finely chopped
3 shallots, chopped
1 garlic clove, finely chopped

Dressing

Juice of 2 limes
1 small dried chilli, finely chopped
1–2 tbs coconut milk
1 tbs palm sugar
Sea salt to taste

Combine all the ingredients, make the dressing, add to the
ingredients and pound together until well mixed.

Serve as a side salad.

Watermelon & green chilli salad

Serves 2

Ingredients
100g each red and white ripe watermelon,
    or any other fruit cut into cubes
3 stems coriander leaves
2 shallots, finely sliced
1 tsp black sesame seed

Dressing
Juice of 1–2 limes
1 tbs palm sugar or to taste
1 small green chilli, finely chopped
Sea salt to taste

Mix all the ingredients together and spoon over the
dressing. Before serving, put the salad in the fridge for
10 minutes to develop the flavours.

Malaysian herbed rice salad

Nasi ulam or 'herbed rice' salad is a favourite dish all over Malaysia, the only country in Southeast Asia to serve the unusual combination of hot rice and shredded herbs, leaves and vegetables. This is a wonderfully tasty, healthy and very different way of eating rice or adding to the chopped vegetable 'rice' prepared by living food purists.

In Malaysia, an extensive variety of locally grown cultivated or wild herbs and edible leaves are added just before serving. Use your imagination and use any kind of shredded herbs, green salad leaves or vegetables that are available.

Ingredients
100g cauliflower, or any other vegetable that can be finely chopped to resemble rice

Herbs & leaves clockwise from bottom
20g each finely shredded fresh gingerflower, pennywort, turmeric leaf, mint, *laksa* leaf, holy basil, cosmos, lemon basil, curry leaf or any available substitutes
1 stem fresh lemongrass, soft inner part finely chopped
2 kaffir lime leaves, shredded
Juice of 1 lime
2 shallots finely sliced
½ cucumber, peeled, seeded & chopped
Palm sugar to taste
1 small red chilli, finely chopped
2 tbs coconut milk
1 tbs crispy onions (see *Tasty Extras*)

Place the chopped vegetable 'rice' in a bowl. Carefully add all the other ingredients. Top with crispy shallots and serve at room temperature. Serve with the following spice dip.

Spice dip
3 small red and green chillies
4 shallots, finely sliced
2 garlic cloves, chopped
2 cm fresh ginger, chopped
1 cm fresh turmeric, chopped
Inside part of 1 lemongrass, chopped
Juice of ½ lime or 1 lime leaf, finely shredded (optional)
Palm sugar to taste
Sea salt to taste

Pound or grind the above together to make a smooth paste and adjust the seasoning to your taste.

Coloured 'rice'

Southeast Asian cooks have many natural ways of colouring local white rice to give it different flavours and make it more appealing. Experiment with colours, add a tablespoon or two of coconut milk and a squeeze of lime juice to keep the 'rice' moist before adding extra leaves, herbs or vegetables.

Blue rice: soak 6 butterfly pea flowers (see *Edible Flowers*) in 5 tablespoons of hot water until the water is bright blue. These small, blue flowers grow wild all over the region and have a very intensive 'pea' taste. Be careful when using them as they can stain hands and clothing! There is no substitute for these flowers (see *Ingredients, Edible Flowers*).

Yellow rice: mix with fresh or powdered turmeric or yellow gardenia flowers (see *Ingredients, Edible Flowers*). Try to buy fresh turmeric, as the powdered form has little or no taste. Onion skins can also be used but the colour and taste will be very mild. Yellow rice can be combined with freshly grated coconut, ginger and shredded herbs.

Red rice: pound 1 tbs annatto seeds (see *Ingredients, Nuts & Seeds*) with 1 tbs water to make a paste, mix 1 tbs or more into the 'living' rice. Red hibiscus flowers (see *Ingredients, Edible Flowers*) or beetroot can also be used.

Green rice: use pandanus, *kayu sugih* (see *Ingredients, Leaves & Herbs*) or spinach leaves. Pandanus leaves have a very specific taste that many dislike, so soak 1 tbs shredded leaves in 2 tbs hot water and try the taste before using.

Black rice: to colour the 'rice' black, use a handful of dried coconut peel and soak in a little hot water.

Brown rice: grate 2 tbs palm sugar and add to 1 tbs water to make brown 'rice'.

Bon Ton *laksa*

Serves 2

Ingredients
100g fresh, thin rice noodles
200 mls coconut milk thinned with 2 tbs water

Soak the rice noodles in the warmed coconut water until soft and 'cooked' through. Take out the noodles, drain and set aside.

Spice paste
Pound or blend the following together to make a paste:
1 tbs cashew nuts, soaked for 3 hours
1 large red chilli, chopped
1 small red chilli, chopped
1 cm fresh galangal, finely sliced
6 small shallots, finely sliced
2 garlic cloves, chopped
2 cm fresh turmeric, peeled & chopped
1 stem fresh lemongrass, outer leaves removed and soft
    inside part finely chopped
Handful of *laksa* leaves, shredded
1 tbs grated palm sugar
Juice of 1 lime
Sea salt to taste

Add the spice paste to the coconut milk and mix together, then the warmed through noodles adjusting the thickness of the sauce to your liking.

Before serving, garnish with beansprouts, more *laksa* leaves, chopped cucumber and pineapple, sliced baby corn, finely sliced gingerflower, crispy onions (see *Tasty Extras*) and a slice of lime.

Penang *mamak* noodles

Serves 2

Mamak is a term used to describe dishes made by Tamil muslims from southern India whose families migrated to Malaysia generations ago. Their food has developed to include many wonderful dishes using elements of all the different kinds of ethnic cuisines in the country. This is a 'living' adaptation of the all time favourite fried Malaysian yellow noodle dish with Indian spices, called Mee India and is served all over Penang.

Ingredients
200g choko or white daikon noodles cut with a vegetable
 noodle machine (see *Utensils*)

Spice paste
3 cm turmeric, chopped
2 shallots, sliced
2 garlic cloves, chopped
¼ tsp cumin seeds
½ tsp coriander seeds
1 tsp ginger, chopped
1-2 tsp palm sugar
Sea salt to taste

Prepare the 'noodles' and set aside. Pound or blend the above spice paste ingredients together, adding some coconut milk and perhaps a little water to thin the paste. Add the 'noodles' into the paste and let stand for 30 minutes before adding the following:
50g firm tofu cut into very small cubes
1 small green chilli, deseeded & finely chopped
A handful of coriander leaves
20g beansprouts
20g spring onions, chopped

Garnish with chopped spring onions & coriander leaves.

Vegetable, herb & glass *bihun* noodles

Serves 2

Ingredients

200g bihun (thin rice noodles) soaked in warm water with
salt until soft. Drain & set aside.

Dressing:

2 inside stems of lemongrass, sliced very finely
2 large kaffir lime leaves, very finely shredded
Juice 1-2 limes
1 tbs honey
1 small red chilli, deseeded & chopped
1-2 tsp sesame oil
Sea salt to taste

Season the dressing according to your taste. Add it to the
noodles and mix in well. Wait for 10 minutes to let the
flavours develop and perhaps adjust the seasoning again.
Just before serving, mix all the shredded ingredients
together, leaving some of the peanuts, curry leaves and
gingerflower to garnish the dish.

Rawfully Good / Templetree & Bon Ton Resort

Clockwise from the top around the rice noodles:

50g white cabbage

50g gingerflower

50g soya bean sprouts

20g turmeric leaf

50g pounded spicy peanuts (see *Tasty Extras*)

½ cucumber, peeled & seeded

2 tbs tamarind, palm sugar & sliced red onions

20g chopped ginger and galangal

Young coconut, mango & shaved ice dessert

Serves 2

This is a healthy 'living' version of a 'straight from the factory' tasting dessert loved by young and old across Southeast Asia.

Although the colouring (seldom food grade!) of the sugar syrups may vary from country to country, condensed milk is still one of the main ingredients!

Ingredients
A mountain of shaved ice per person
2 young coconuts, flesh cut into bite-sized pieces
A few spoons of fresh coconut water
4 tbs palm sugar
2 mangoes, peeled & cubed

Mix the coconut water and palm sugar to make a syrup. Shave or crush the ice and quickly make a mountain. Put this in the centre of 2 bowls, with the cubed mango and coconut meat around. Drizzle with the palm sugar and coconut water syrup and serve immediately.

Laos

L'Elephant Restaurant, Luang Prabang

F lying into Luang Prabang, a protected world heritage site since 1995, for the first time, I was reminded of Heidelberg. These towns, both picturesque centers of learning built on the banks of stately rivers are gradually being steamrollered by mass tourism. Luang Prabang, however, still manages to remain in a kind of gentle time warp. The slow pace of life on the Mekong influences the tourist hordes who seem to be more hushed and sedate than elsewhere.

Laotian food is not as spicy or sweet as Thai food. It is a down-to-earth cuisine with complex flavours. Seasonal, fresh, wild jungle foods abound, especially in the north of the country. Being part of French Indochina for more than half a century influenced the everyday food of Laos. Coffee and baguettes could even be found in Luang Prabang, a town dedicated to royal cuisine – the monarchy resided here until the Communist revolution in 1975. Recipes collected by Chaleunsilp Phia Sing (c. 1898-1967), the last famous royal chef and master of ceremonies to the court in Luang Prabang, was published in 1981.

The town's daily markets are filled with vendors selling beetles by the tin, rats, squirrels, eels, strange-looking river fish and buckets of *padek*, the thick, purple, frothing fermented fish sauce beloved by Laotians, taking the meaning of 'living' food to a new level! At the same time, I was amazed at the array of unusual wild vegetables, herbs and leaves on sale at the markets. These provided the basic ingredients for the dishes in this chapter.

Yannick Upravan, one of Lao's foremost chefs and restaurateurs, was born in Luang Prabang, left during the political turmoil in the mid 1970s, trained as a chef in France, met his partner Gilles Vautrin there and returned with him to open L'Elephant, a gourmet French restaurant in his grandmother's colonial town house.

Although his heart and taste buds are firmly anchored in traditional French cuisine, Yannick and his partner source the best possible local ingredients and incorporate local herbs and flavours. Because it was difficult to source the produce he needed for his restaurant, Yannick began to plant his own herbs and vegetables. The farm has now expanded and the surplus produce is sold to other hotels and restaurants in the area. A brand new project, on which I am collaborating, is L'Elephant Vert, which will be the first ethno-botanical restaurant in Southeast Asia. It will open in October 2010.

Contact: L'Elephant Restaurant & L'Elephant Vert cuisine ethnobotanique
Luang Prabang, Lao PDR
Telephone: 856 71 252 482 Fax: 856 71 252 492
Email: contact@elephant-restau.com Web: www.elefant-restau.com

Luang Prabang market soup

Serves 2

Ingredients

1 bunch each Thai holy and sweet basils, leaves chopped
1 bunch wild baby rocket, chopped
1 bunch coriander, stems & roots chopped, leaves whole
1 bunch Vietnamese mint or *laksa*, leaves only
1 bunch spearmint, leaves only
100g baby kalian or broccoli
100g spinach, chopped
20g Lao hog plums or 1 tsp fresh orange juice mixed
      with 1 tbs fresh lime juice and ½ tsp sea salt
1 small green chilli, deseeded & finely chopped
3 stems water spinach or morning glory, leaves & stems
      finely chopped
50g watercress, roughly chopped
20g Lao chrysanthemum leaves, chopped
50g snow peas, chopped
3-4 tbs coconut milk
1 tsp sea salt or to taste
2 tbs snow pea tendrils for decoration

Roughly chop all the above ingredients apart from the
snow pea tendrils. Blend together with coconut milk and
perhaps some coconut water to make a thick soup.
Put in the fridge for an hour so that the flavours can
develop. Remove from the fridge and adjust the seasoning.

To serve

Serve at room temperature decorated with snow tea
tendrils, slices of baby corn, herbs, garlic chive flowers
and grated carrot.

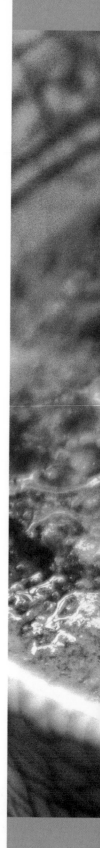

Lao green papaya salad

Serves 2

Ingredients
8 different coloured baby aubergines, finely sliced
2 stems of bitterfruit herb or tarragon, leaves only
1 small green papaya, finely grated
4 cherry tomatoes, quartered
2 young heads of garlic, crushed or 2 garlic cloves, minced

Dressing
Juice of 1-2 limes
1 large red chilli, deseeded & chopped
Juice of 1 Lao hog plum or 1 tsp fresh orange juice mixed
    with 1 tbs lime juice & pinch of salt
2 tbs palm sugar, grated
½ tsp sea salt or to taste

Slice the aubergines and soak for 30 minutes in salty
water to take away the bitterness. Drain well and pat dry.
Prepare the other ingredients and the dressing.
Before serving adjust the salty, sweet and sour flavours
of the dressing before adding to the salad.
Mix well and serve immediately.

Lao watercress
& green algae salad

Serves 2

Ingredients

200g fresh watercress, roughly chopped
100g Lao dried algae, soaked overnight, drained & rolled
   into small balls or fresh green seaweed in small pieces
20g sawtooth coriander
20g fresh coriander leaves
50g fresh waterspinach leaves
6 Lao figs or 4 fresh European figs, sliced
50g wild Lao spinach or 100g green spinach, chopped
4 large slices of pineapple to serve

Dressing

4 tbs pineapple puree
2 tbs lime juice
2 tbs palm sugar
½ tsp salt
1 tbs black sesame seeds
1 tbs thick coconut milk

Chop all the salad ingredients and prepare the dressing.
Just before serving, mix everything together carefully, add
some of the sesame seeds (leaving some for decoration)
and heap carefully onto thick slices of pineapple, 1 per
person. Sprinkle sesame seeds over the salad, together with
some more herbs and chopped chilli.

Lao style mushroom *laab*

Serves 2

Ingredients
400g carefully cleaned mushrooms
100g baby bok choy, finely sliced
50g bitterleaf or tarragon, leaves only
100g beansprouts or any kind of sprouts
20g Lao orange, chopped or
10g tangerine zest
4 sprigs of mint, leaves only
50g garlic chives, chopped
20g sawtooth coriander, shredded
20g sweet Thai basil

Chop the cleaned mushrooms very finely and drizzle with lime juice to stop them going black. Prepare the remaining ingredients and add the orange just before serving.

Dressing
Juice of 2 Lao hog plums or the flesh of ½ tangerine
2 tbs palm sugar
¼ tsp Lao or Szechuan peppercorns, crushed
1 dried red chilli, finely chopped & seeds removed
2 tbs crispy rice powder (see *Tasty Extras*)
2 tbs crispy onions (see *Tasty Extras*)

Combine all the above together apart from the rice powder and onions. Adjust the seasoning.

To serve
Add a generous handful of Laotian *kroeng* ham or mixed aromatic herbs such as coriander, Asian basils, more mint and chives to the salad together with the dressing just before serving.

Lao edible flower & leaf salad

Serves 2

Ingrdients

Here we used some of the many wild and cultured Lao edible flowers and leaves, but use any alternatives (see *Edible Flowers*) such as pansies, borage or nasturtiums and any herbs or leaves that may be available.

Edible flowers

50g each yellow & white Chinese baby kalian flowers
20g butterfly pea flowers & pea tendrils, stamens removed
10 sprigs of basil flowers, taken off the stems
10 tiny yellow bitterflowers
10 baby banana flower stamens
10 tuberose petals, stamens removed
20 each red & white bean flowers, petals only

Prepare and mix all the flowers together, remove the stamens and use only single petals.

Edible leaves

20g pea tendrils & young leaves
20g passionfruit tendrils & young leaves
20g Lao ruccola or baby wild ruccola
20g Asian clover
20g sawtooth coriander
3 stems coriander, leaves only
20g Vietnamese mint, leaves only
20g chrysanthemum leaves

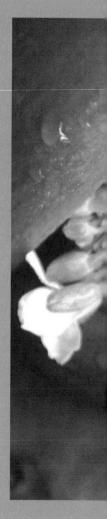

Dressing

1-2 dried chillies, seeds removed & finely chopped
1-2 tbs palm sugar
1-2 tbs lime juice
1 tsp salt

Mix all the above ingredients well, perhaps adding a little more palm sugar to offset the bitterness of some of the flowers and leaves. Adjust the seasoning to your taste.

To serve

Combine all the flowers and leaves and mix together. Just before serving pour over the dressing and toss carefully. Serve immediately.

Green & white salad

Serves 2

Ingredients
½ long green Chinese lettuce, leaves & roots finely shredded
2 small yams, peeled & shredded
2 tiny young bamboo shoots, outside peeled off & sliced
Inside part of two lemongrass stems, very finely sliced
20g fresh dill or to taste
4 large white hummingbird flowers, petals only
1 large green chilli, seeds removed & finely chopped

Prepare the above and mix together.

Dressing
1 tbs tamarind pulp, mixed with water & sieved
6 slices dried bael fruit (soaked in 2 cups of water
    overnight to give 2 tbs juice) or alternatively mix juice of
    ½ lime with 1 tbs tangerine juice
1 tbs palm sugar
½ tsp white pepper, ground
1 tsp sea salt or to taste

Prepare the dressing, adjust the seasoning and mix into
the salad just before serving.

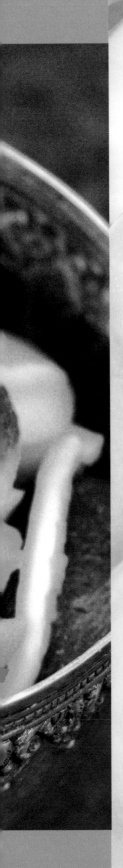

Lao fruit salad with sweet & sour sauce

Serves 2

This simple dessert is made with fruit that will be very difficult to find outside Laos or North Thailand, so just use any tropical fruits that have different textures and colours to achieve nearly the same effect!

Ingredients
1 young coconut, flesh cut into strips
100g ripe papaya cut into bite size pieces
2 ripe milkfruit, peeled, seeds removed & sliced
1 large green guava, seeds removed & sliced
3 hog plums, inner seed removed & chopped

Prepare the fruit and set aside.

Sweet and sour sauce
Juice of 6 hogplums or 2 tbs lime juice
   and 1 tbs tangerince juice
A pinch of salt
1-2 tbs palm sugar
1 tbs Lao sesame or black sesame seeds

Make the dressing and check that it has a balance of sweet and sour flavours.
Sprinkle over the sesame seed just before serving.

Lao condiments

Centre
Dried large red chillies,
fresh large red & small red chillies

Clockwise from top right
Sea salt
Coriander seeds
Ground rice powder
Crispy onions (see *Tasty Extras*)
Lao or Szechuan pepper

Cambodia

Hotel de la Paix, Siem Reap

Expecting to find Cambodia still living in the shadows of its recent history, I was surprised when I arrived in Siem Reap to be greeted instead with ghostly glimpses of Angkor Wat through the rain and a majestic drive into the city down bustling roads lined with huge ancient trees.

In the last ten years, stability has come to the country, tourists from all over the world are flocking back, more temples are being restored and most importantly, there is a very strong movement to revive the cultural and culinary heritage that disappeared along with the lost generation. This century's political turmoil left no time to think about how important it was to keep Khmer cuisine alive and only recently, now that peace and prosperity have at last returned to the country, can young local chefs rediscover their culinary heritage.

Cambodian or Khmer food has always been influenced from many directions: from the kingdoms of ancient Java during the era of temple building, from India, by immigrants from China and most recently because the country was a part of French colonial history. Many people appreciate Cambodian cuisine and believe that it is superior to Thai, it has more complex salty and bitter flavours, is less spicy and is never as sweet. Although many of the basic dishes are similar to those of neighbouring Thailand, Vietnam and Laos, Khmer cuisine it is not as well known or documented and the unique combination of ingredients used in some of the *kroeung* or basic spice pastes can only be found here.

I had come to Siem Reap to work with Joannes Riviere, the author of a recent book about Cambodian cuisine and the Executive Chef at the Hotel de la Paix. The hotel, a spacious Art Deco style building that has played a significant role in the history of the city, is strategically located near the centre of Siem Reap within easy walking distance of the main tourist restaurant and shopping areas. The cool designer restaurant, built around a courtyard with a shady banyan tree in the centre, is a relaxing haven of peace to return to after dusty, hot days spent wandering around the many temples. The hotel's owners are active in supporting community charities and guests are encouraged to visit the various projects and help where possible.

As well as taking me to explore the produce to be found at the most important daily markets around the city, Joannes took me to meet some enterprising local farmers who are starting to grow an increasing amount of 'organic' produce to supply the rising demand from the many new restaurants and hotels in this city of new found prosperity.

Contact: Hotel de la Paix, Sivutha Boulevard, Siem Reap, Kingdom of Cambodia
Telephone: +855 (0)63 966 000 Fax: +855 (0) 63 966 001
Email: info@hoteldelapaixangkor.com Web: www.hoteldelapaixangkor.com

Towers of Angkor green tomato soup

Serves 2

Ingredients

1 large, medium ripe mango, peeled & chopped
4 green tomatoes, chopped
1 small pineapple, peeled & chopped
Inside of 2 stems of lemongrass, chopped
3 shallots, chopped
2 garlic cloves, chopped
4 lime leaves, shredded
2 chilli leaves, shredded
1 tsp fresh turmeric, chopped
1 tsp fresh Chinese keys, chopped
Juice of 1 lime
1-2 tbs palm sugar
½ tsp salt
2 tbs coconut milk for decoration

Blend the above ingredients together, leaving some pineapple wedges and slices of green tomato for decoration. Adjust the seasoning and put in the fridge for 30 minutes to let the flavours develop.
Remove from the fridge and check the seasoning again. Serve at room temperature decorated with 'towers' of pineapple, slices of green tomato, slivers of red chilli and drizzles of coconut milk.

Straw & oyster mushroom salad

Serves 2

Ingredients
200g fresh mixed mushrooms, carefully cleaned, dried
    & drizzled with lime juice to prevent them going black
2 tbs palm sugar
Juice of 2 limes
50g fresh lotus root, peeled & sliced very thinly
2 shallots, finely sliced
2 tbs fresh peanuts, skins removed
2 tbs young tamarind leaf stalks
2 stalks lemon basil, leaves only
½ tsp sea salt or to taste
2 tsp dried chilli flakes

Make a marinade with the palm sugar and lime juice,
add the mushrooms and palm sugar and leave for about
15 minutes so that they can absorb the flavours.
Check the seasoning of the dressing before adding the
other ingredients. Garnish with chilli flakes and serve at
once.

Cucumber rolls with three spicy fillings

Serves 2

Ingredients
3 small cucumbers, some of the skin peeled off lengthways to make a pattern
Cut into 2 cm thick slices, seeds removed

Rice paddy herb filling
1 garlic clove
1 small red chilli
2 shallots
1-2 tsp palm sugar
½ tsp sea salt or to taste
1 tbs chives, chopped
1 tsp rice paddy herb, leaves only or ¼ tsp cumin powder
1 unripe guava, peeled & chopped
Rice paddy herb or chives for decoration

Pound or blend the above together and adjust the seasoning.

Laksa leaf filling
100g green tamarind pods
1 garlic clove, chopped
20 *laksa* or Vietnamese mint leaves
1 tbs palm sugar
½ tsp ground white pepper
½ tsp sea salt or to taste
Vietnamese mint leaves for decoration

Pound or blend the above together and adjust the seasoning.

Coriander and green peppercorn filling

Inside of 4 stems of lemongrass, chopped
1 tsp fresh green pepper
½ tsp salt or to taste
2 lime leaves, finely shredded
2 sawtooth coriander leaves or coriander leaves
2 tbs green mango, chopped
1-2 tsp palm sugar
Small sprig of green peppercorns for decoration

Pound or blend the above together to make a thick paste
and adjust the seasoning.

To serve

Stuff 2 slices of cucumber per person with each of the
fillings and decorate with the respective herbs or green
peppercorns. Serve immediately.

Lotus & herb salad

Serves 2

Ingredients
1 lotus flower, stamens removed,
    use petals only
100g thin purple lotus stem, cut on the
    cross into thin slices
2 shallots, thinly sliced
10 chilli leaves, shredded
1 tbs Chinese celery, leaves only
1 tbs green part of spring onion, chopped
5 pink or white vegetable hummingbird
    flower, stamens removed, use petals
    only, or any other edible flowers

Dressing
1 tbs fresh galangal, finely chopped
1 small red chilli, deseeded & chopped
2 tbs tamarind paste soaked in 1 tbs water
1-2 tbs palm sugar
½ tsp sea salt or to taste

Prepare the salad ingredients and set aside. Make the dressing
and adjust the seasoning to your taste. Just before serving,
add the dressing to the salad and toss carefully.
Serve at once.

Yam millefeuille with butterfly pea sauce

Serves 2

Ingredients
2 large yams, peeled & sliced very thinly with a mandoline
40 or more whole spinach, coriander, holy basil leaves or
    herbs of your choice
Salt & pepper to taste

Slice the yam very thinly and stack, putting herbs or leaves
and some sauce between each slice. Season to taste.

Butterfly pea sauce
4 butterfly pea flowers
50g white sesame seeds
2 tbs coconut milk
½ tsp ground white pepper
Juice 1 lime
½ tsp salt or to taste

Soak the blue flowers in 2 tbs hot water for 30 minutes.
Discard the flowers and keep the water. Pound or blend the
sesame seeds together with the other ingredients and add
the blue water to the paste to make a sauce. The water will
have a very intensive pea flavour, so adjust to your taste and
season.

To serve
Carefully trim the yam and leaf stack into a square, put
some of the sauce on a plate with the yam on top.
Garnish with another pea flower or herbs of your choice.

Rawfully Good / Hotel de la Paix

210

Cambodian spice paste

Serves 2

Ingredients

This is the basic Cambodian curry spice paste used in the kitchens at the Hotel de la Paix. Note that no salt is listed in the ingredients and that this should be added when the actual dish has been prepared.

Inner part of 2 stems lemongrass, finely chopped
2 tbs fresh turmeric, chopped
2 tbs fresh galangal, chopped
1 tbs fresh Chinese keys, chopped
2 lime leaves, shredded
2 cloves of garlic, chopped
2 shallots, chopped

Pound or grind all the above ingredients together to make a thick, fragrant paste to use in for all kinds of salads and soups.

Mango & lemon basil dessert

Serves 2

Ingredients
2 large ripe but still firm mangoes
1 small bunch lemon basil, leaves only

Mango and kguy sauce
1 tsp fresh turmeric, finely chopped
100g Cambodian kguy fruit, seeds removed, fruit pulp only
   or 4 tbs tangerine juice mixed with 2 tbs lime juice
2 tbs palm sugar or to taste
Spring water

Blend the above ingredients together to make a thick sauce
and adjust the seasoning. Slice the mango with a mandoline
so that each person has 3 large slices. Drizzle the mango
slices with some of the sauce, cover with lemon basil leaves
and roll up.

To serve
Put some sauce on each plate, place 3 mango rolls on top,
drizzle with more sauce and garnish with lemon basil leaves.

Vietnam

Ninh Van Bay, a Six Senses Hideaway, Nha Trang

W hen Eva, a successful Swedish fashion model, met Old Etonian Sonu Shivdasani at the Monaco Grand Prix in 1986, little did they know what life had in store for them. They visited the Maldives on holiday together and fell in love with Baa Atoll, where they consequently leased the largest island to build their first unique, beautifully simple but very sophisticated and environmentally sustainable resort, Soneva Fushi.

Retaining the original concept that reflected and supported their ever-increasing ecological awareness, Sonu and Eva have worked tirelessly to create many other resorts

all over the world. Now Sonu watches over the management side and Eva is the creative director plus environmental and ethical conscience, completing existing and working on new projects with her amazing eye and attention to fine detail.

Because I was looking for Vietnamese recipes to adapt for this book, Eva suggested that I spend some time with Chef David Thai at the Six Senses Hideaway at Ninh Van Bay off the coast of Nha Trang in Central Vietnam. Accessible only by boat, this remote and very secluded hideaway has a choice of spacious and beautifully designed villas to choose from – built into the rocks, over the sea, or on the mountainside overlooking the bay. The resort also has a large and very well-stocked organic garden making it very easy for me to be able to go there at any time to pick all the fresh, pesticide-free herbs, Southeast Asian vegetables and salads that David and I needed for our week of experimenting with 'living' food dishes.

Nha Trang is a bustling fishing town 400 km north of Saigon with some interesting monuments to visit. When Vietnam's last Emperor Bao Dai built a private villa overlooking the bay, Nha Trang became well known but it was not until Six Senses opened Evason Ana Mandara, the first luxury resort in the country on Nha Trang's beautiful beach in 1997, that the town was suddenly a tourist destination.

David and I spent a happy day together exploring the two large daily markets in Nha Trang to find more unusual produce to add to the selection available from the resort garden. Leaving the stalls selling endangered dried seahorses and a huge range of other sad sea creatures behind us, I also avoided the buckets of homemade, evil smelling fish pastes and *nuoc mam* fish sauce. We had a rest at a stall selling freshly-made pennywort juice, marvelled at the huge variety of spring roll wrappers on sale,

Rawfully Good / Ninh Van Bay

the many different shredded salads and all the spice pastes freshly prepared every morning for busy housewives to take-away.

Fresh herbs are used more than root spices in this part of Vietnam and plastic buckets full of different kinds of mint, basils, coriander, sawtooth coriander and dill (collectively known as *rau thom* or fragrant herbs), together with little bowls of chopped chillies in vinegar, white sugar and fried peanuts are placed on the tables so that hungry guests can add and mix in their preferred flavours to each dish.

To the astonishment of kitchen staff, our 'rawfully good' canapeés using different versions of Vietnamese pennywort and the 'tasting' dinner to follow were a great success especially with those guests who had never considered trying 'living' food before. Guests and staff were amazed that we were able to serve authentic Vietnamese-tasting dishes without using fish sauce or animal products of any kind, just by adding more herbs and spices to balance and create the usual Vietnamese flavours.

Contact: Six Senses Hideaway, Ninh Van Bay, Ninh Hoa, Khanh Hoa, Vietnam
Telephone: (+84) 58 372 8222 Fax: (+84) 58 372 8223
Email: reservations-ninhvan@sixsenses.com
Web: www.sixsenses.com/six-senses-hideaway-ninh-van-bay

'Living' *pho*

Serves 2

Ingredients
1 kg tomatoes, deseeded & chopped
2 shallots, sliced
4 straw mushrooms, chopped
4 stems Chinese celery, chopped
1 tbs coriander roots, chopped
1 tbs Vietnamese mint, leaves only,
    chopped with more for garnish
1 tbs rice paddy herb, chopped
1 tbs fresh ginger, chopped
1 tbs fresh galangal, chopped
2 star aniseed seeds
1 tsp sea salt
1 tsp white pepper
4 tbs spring water
100g fresh glass noodles
2 straw mushrooms per person, sliced in half
2 baby bok choy or spinach, shredded
Fresh herbs and crispy onions (see *Tasty Extras*) to garnish

Pound or blend tomatoes, then add the other ingredients.
Strain through cheesecloth overnight and add enough
water to make a thin, clear soup. Adjust the seasoning.
Soak the glass noodles in warm water until soft, add to
the soup, together with 2 straw mushrooms per person.

To serve
Top the soup with a handful of fresh herbs, bok choy or
spinach, more finely chopped tomatoes and a sprinkle of
crispy onions.

Fresh amaranth rolls
with spicy tomato sauce

Serves 2

Ingredients

3 large leaves of red amaranth or spinach per person
150g fresh herbs & edible leaves:
    dill, Thai basil, lemon basil, coriander, onion chives
    or whatever is available
100g cos lettuce, shredded or baby salad leaves
2 shallots, sliced
4 cherry tomatoes, chopped
1 tbs crispy onions
6 long garlic chives to tie the rolls together

Prepare all the herbs, tomatoes and just before serving roll
up in the spinach leaves and tie with a chive.

Spicy tomato sauce

2 large tomatoes, deseeded & chopped
1 small red chilli, deseeded & chopped
2 shallots, chopped
1 garlic clove, chopped
1 tsp fresh galangal, chopped
½ tsp coriander seeds
Juice of 1 lime
1-2 tbs coconut milk
Sea salt to taste

Pound or blend the above ingredients, adding enough
coconut milk at the end to make a smooth paste. Sieve the
mixture again if you prefer to have an even smoother
sauce. Adjust the seasoning before serving.

Ninh Van Bay 'living' noodles

Serves 2

Ingredients daikon 'noodles'

200g daikon radish peeled & cut into 'noodles'
    with the spiral machine (see *Utensils*) and
    soaked in salty water for 30 minutes
1 large red chilli, deseeded & chopped
20g garlic chives, chopped
3 shallots, finely sliced

Dressing

1tbs fresh galangal, chopped
1tbs fresh ginger, chopped
2 tbs coconut milk
Juice of 1-2 limes
1 tbs orange juice
1 tbs palm sugar
Sea salt to taste

Pound or blend the above together to make a paste.
Use the coconut milk, orange and lime juice to thin the
paste to a dressing. Prepare the noodles then drain well
before combining with the remaining ingredients.
Mix well together and adjust the seasoning.

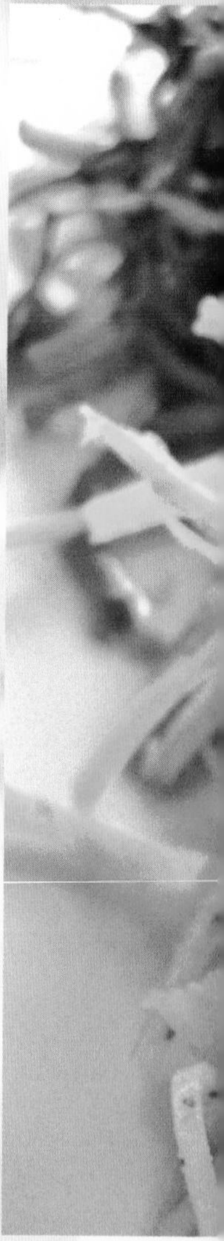

Carrot 'noodles'

200g carrot 'noodles' made with the
    spiral machine (see *Utensils*)
50g bean sprouts
50g chopped, mixed herbs, roughly
    chopped
50g spring onions, chopped

Dressing

1 small green chilli, deseeded & chopped
1 tbs palm sugar
Juice 1 lime
½ tsp coriander seed
½ tsp salt

Grind or blend the above together to
make a paste, thin with more lime juice
and adjust the seasoning. Just before
serving, mix the in the dressing.

Yellow 'pumpkin' noodles

200g yellow pumpkin peeled and cut
    into 'noodles' using the spiral
    machine (see *Utensils*) and soaked
    in cold, salty water for 30 minutes.
50g cucumber, peeled & cubed
20g crispy onions (see *Tasty Extras*)

Dressing

1-2 tsp virgin coconut oil
1 small green and 1 small red chilli, seeds taken out
    & finely chopped
2 tbs spearmint leaves, shredded
1 large lime leaf, shredded
Juice of 1-2 limes
1-2 tbs palm sugar
Sea salt to taste

Prepare the noodles and the dressing and just before
serving pour over the dressing and mix well.

Fresh Vietnamese handroll

Serves 4

Ingredients

1 pkt large, square Vietnamese rice papers, dipped in warm
    water and put on a cloth to keep moist
4 pieces of raw nori sheets
300g rice vermicelli, soaked until soft & drained well
500g chopped, mixed green herbs, edible leaves & vegetables
100g white cabbage, shredded
1 large red chilli, deseeded & chopped

Place the first two rice papers side by side on a large, damp
cloth, overlapping them by about 5 cm. Place the nori
seaweed sheets on the top and cover with the vermicelli,
chilli, herbs and cabbage. Season and roll up not too tightly.
Keep alternating layers of herbs and rice papers until the
roll is about 12 cm in diameter. Season each layer lightly
with salt and pepper. Roll up in clingfilm and leave in the
fridge for at least 1 hour to let the flavours develop.
Cut into thick rounds through the clingfilm.
Remove and serve with the dipping sauce.

Dipping sauce

2 tbs palm sugar
1 large green and red chilli, deseeded & chopped
2 tbs lime juice
1 tbs coriander root, chopped
1 tbs coriander leaves
1 tbs Vietnamese mint or *laksa* leaves, chopped
1 tbs shallots, finely sliced
½ tsp white pepper
½ -1 tsp salt to taste

Pound or blend all the ingredients together and mix in the
sliced shallots just before serving. Adjust the seasoning.

Baby vegetable salad

Serves 2

Ingredients
2 of the following for each person cherry tomatoes, baby bell peppers, baby zucchini, button mushrooms, shitake mushrooms, large red and green chillies.

Cut the tops off the cherry tomatoes and the baby bell peppers and discard the seeds. Cut the baby zucchini in half lengthways and scrape out the seeds with a teaspoon. Cut the stems out of the mushrooms and drizzle with lemon juice. Cut the stalks of the large chillies, cut in half lengthways and take out the seeds and membrane.

Salad
4 stalks Vietnamese mint or *laksa* leaf, leaves only
4 stalks spearmint, leaves only
4 stalks coriander, roots chopped, leaves left whole
2 stalks Chinese celery, leaves only
2 shallots
1 garlic clove
1 tsp galangal
1 lime leaf, shredded
½ tsp lime zest
1 tbs palm sugar
1 small red chilli, deseeded & chopped
Juice 1 lime
Pinch star aniseed powder
1 tsp sea salt or to taste
Chop all the above ingredients and spices and mix well together. Adjust the seasoning to your taste.

To serve
Just before serving stuff all the baby vegetables with the salad mixture and serve immediately.

Purple potato & beetroot salad

Serves 2

This is not a completely 'raw' dish because the potatoes are slightly steamed but the result is so beautiful that it had to be included!

Ingredients
2 purple potatoes, peeled, sliced & soaked in water
    with a pinch of salt to remove some of the starch
2 baby beetroot, peeled & sliced or chopped
2 tbs baby salad leaves, chopped herbs or sprouts

Dressing
2 passionfruit, juice only, leaving a few seeds for decoration
½ ripe mango, chopped
Juice of 1 lime
1 tbs palm sugar or to taste
½ tbs sea salt
½ tbs white pepper

Gently steam the purple potato slices over hot water until soft. Make the dressing. Prepare the baby beetroot and add to the dressing. Leave in the fridge for 30 minutes to let the flavours develop. Adjust the seasoning.

To serve
Put two or three potato slices on a plate, top with the beetroot and then the herbs and sprouts. Drizzle over some more dressing.

Vegetable & herb paste on sugarcane or lemongrass

Serves 2

Ingredients

4 sugarcane or lemongrass sticks
300g very finely chopped mixed vegetables such as
    carrots, tomatoes, bell peppers, spinach, mushrooms
    or whatever you would like to use
50g fresh mixed herbs, finely chopped
1 tsp palm sugar
1 small red chilli, deseeded & chopped
½ tsp white pepper
½ tsp sea salt or to taste
½ tsp agar powder
1 tbs mixed black & white sesame seeds

Chop all the vegetables and the herbs very finely. Mix the
agar powder with 1 tbs water and heat gently until the
powder has dissolved. Set aside and when the mixture is
just beginning to set, add it to the chopped herbs and
vegetables, mix well and put in the fridge to set.
After 1 hour wet your hands and press small handfuls of
the mixture around the sugarcane or lemongrass sticks.
Roll in the black and white sesame seeds and put back in
the fridge until ready to serve. Serve with 'living' sweet
chilli sauce (see Tasty Extras).

Tropical fruit & pennywort terrine

Serves 2

Ingredients

¼ tsp agar powder mixed with 2 tbs of any kind of sweet
herb (here we used pennywort) or pure fruit juice
100g each different coloured, finely sliced fruit such as
strawberries melon, mango, dragon fruit or whatever
you would like to use

Mix the juice and agar powder together and stir until
the powder has dissolved. Baste the bottom and sides of
a small, rectangular or other form with a thin layer of
neutral vegetable oil. Spoon the first layer of jelly into the
form, put into the fridge and wait for it to set. Repeat,
adding layers until the bottom layer of jelly is about 2 cm
thick. Now add a layer of fruit, mixing the colours, top
with a layer of jelly and so on, until the form is full.
Cover and put in the fridge overnight to set through
completely. Just before serving, turn out carefully and cut
into thick slices. Perhaps make a simple fruit puree sauce
with a tablespoon of coconut milk added and spoon
around the slices of terrine.

Mangosteen & lemongrass sorbet

Serves 2

Ingredients

1 kg mangosteen, seeds removed and flesh pureed with
100 mls spring water
1 tsp lime juice
1 tsp honey
2 stalks fresh lemongrass

Carefully open the mangosteens, remove the fruit, take
out the seeds and puree it in a blender together with
some water, lime juice and honey. Finely slice the inside
parts of 2 lemon-grass stems, slice finely and blend.
Strain and add to the mangosteen puree. Put in an ice
cream or sorbet machine and process according to the
manufacturers instructions.

vege

couched amaranth in superior

souffed lux

大華

MAJESTIC
RESTAURANT

Singapore

New Majestic Restaurant, Chinatown

L
oh Yik Peng, one of Singapore's most eminent young entrepreneurs, took over and renovated old shops in the centre of Singapore's Chinatown enabling him to open the first small, luxury hotel in the area. The New Majestic Hotel perfectly illustrates how a new generation of local visionaries has come to terms with centuries of colonial heritage, while still managing to keep the balance between conservation, creative international design and all the creature comforts expected by

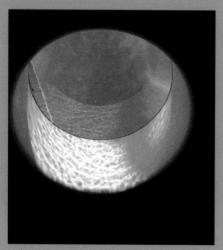

today's discerning travellers. Each room at the hotel is a refreshingly different showcase for local artists and well-known designers. He also teamed up with Chef Yong Bing Ngen, formerly Chef de Cuisine at the legendary Raffles Hotel and Executive Chef at the Jade Restaurant at the Fullerton Hotel to work on the award-winning Majestic Restaurant and Majestic Bar.

The restaurant interior incorporates soothing coloured fabrics with carefully chosen pieces of art from East and West. Combining both traditional and sometimes surprising modern design elements, such as portholes let into the ceiling that look up into the Majestic Hotel's first floor swimming pool, these are reflected in Chef Yong's innovative cuisine, prepared for all to see in the first ever display kitchen to be found in a Chinese fine-dining restaurant in the city.

Having eaten there on a number of occasions, I knew that I had found the Chinese chef I was looking for, one who prepared simply plated, modern Cantonese dishes with a traditional soul and who could perhaps be interested in preparing some 'living' dishes. When I approached him, Chef Yong was hesitant at first but eventually agreed to go with me to the market in Chinatown. When he realized that so much of the produce on offer – lotus root, jasmine buds or flowering Chinese cabbage – could be eaten raw, he became more and more interested and we bought samples of everything to experiment with in the kitchen.

Back at the Majestic Restaurant, the kitchen staff were wondering why Chef had suddenly bought so many different kinds of fresh vegetables. Discussing the possibilities of perhaps including small dishes of the palate-cleansing salads we had created between the courses of his future set menus, he was talking excitedly, deftly wielding his huge clever to cut paper thin slices of lotus root and slivers of tiny kalamansi limes without looking at his hands at all.

Contact: New Majestic Restaurant 31-37 Bukit Pasoh Rd, Chinatown, Singapore 089845
Telephone: +65 6222 3377 Fax: + 65 6223 0907
Email: restaurant@newmajestichotel.com Web: www.newmajestichotel.com

Rawfully Good / New Majestic Restaurant

Jasmine flower & vegetable salad

Serves 2

Ingredients
1 bunch pea shoots & tendrils
3 tbs fresh jasmine flowers, petals only
4 tbs Chinese mustard cabbage, finely sliced
1 small bunch edible chrysanthemum leaves,
    leaves only, chopped
50g red spinach (amaranth) or green spinach,
    leaves only, chopped
1 kalamansi lime, very finely sliced

Prepare the above but do not mix until just before serving.

Dressing
1 tbs good sesame oil
1 tbs tamari sauce
1 tbs palm sugar
1 tbs white sesame seed
Juice of 1 kalamansi lime or the juice of ½ lime
    & 1 tbs tangerine juice with ¼ tsp salt

Make a dressing with the above ingredients and leave for
20 minutes to let the flavours infuse. Check the seasoning
again before mixing into the salad. Serve immediately.

Lotus root with tasty greens

Serves 2

Ingredients
½ fresh lotus root, peeled & sliced very thinly
   with a mandolin
½ yam, peeled & cut into matchsticks
100g wild asparagus, tailed & sliced
4 lady fingers or okra, sliced
1 small bunch spinach, leaves only, chopped

Prepare the above but do not mix until just before serving.

Dressing
1 tbs raw honey
½ tsp Szechuan peppercorns
1 tsp fresh ginger, chopped
3 garlic cloves, very finely chopped
½ tsp sea salt or to taste
Spring water

Prepare the dressing and adjust the seasoning according to
your taste. Just before serving, toss the dressing carefully
into the salad and serve immediately.

Chef Yong's Singapore fruit salad with aloe vera sauce

Serves 2

Ingredients

1 small ripe rock melon
1 dragon fruit
1 pomegranate
4 ripe baby mangoes or
100g ripe mango

Cut the rock melon in half, remove the seeds and cut some of the flesh into cubes and save some of the flesh for the sauce. Peel the dragon fruit and cut into cubes. Break the pomegranate into pieces and take out the seeds, trying to reserve the juice. Cut the mangoes or mangoes into cubes.

Sauce

1 tbs fresh aloe vera pulp
1 tbs palm sugar
Juice of ½ lime
2 tbs avocado puree
2 tbs rockmelon puree

Scrape the aloe vera pulp off the leaves and mix with all the other ingredients, making sure that the sauce is not too bitter. Just before serving, mix all the ingredients together and serve immediately in the two melon halves.

Myanmar

The Strand Hotel, Yangon

B uilt on the banks of the Yangon River in the late 19th century, this gracious old building has undergone many renovations and seen many radical changes since it was opened in 1901 as an hotel by the first luxury hoteliers of note in Southeast Asia, the Sarkies brothers. They were responsible for some of the most prestigious and illustrious hotels in the region, the Raffles in Singapore, the Eastern & Oriental in Penang, Malaysia, and the Hotel Majapahit in Surabaya, Indonesia. But The Strand, the most famous of them all, was mentioned in Murray's *Handbook for Travellers in India, Burma and Ceylon* as 'the finest hostelry East of Suez'.

At that time, Rangoon was one of the most important cities in the then British Empire and because the city was a half-way point between British India and Singapore, The Strand became a 'home from home' to traders and a new breed of rich English who were travelling purely for pleasure. Two World Wars came and went and the hotel opened again in 1945. It was taken over, gutted and returned to its former glory when it became an Aman resort in 1994 and has been managed by GHM Hotels since 1999.

The Strand Bar is still the busiest bar in the city on Friday nights and the Strand Café is a favourite place for visitors to relax and enjoy The Strand's famous Myanmar High Tea after touring the sights of the city.

There are too many wonderful sights to see in Yangon, but for me the city's wholesale market was the most interesting of all the ones I visited in Southeast Asia. There was an Indian man standing in the middle of a huge basket piled waist-high with tiny hot chillies and a Chinese spice seller standing in front of a ginger mountain at least 3 metres high, rows of fresh soy bean sprouts growing out of dark tubs and evil-smelling piles of bamboo shoots. Above all, more green vegetables than I have ever seen anywhere in the region helped to complete the amazing scene.

According to some Myanmar culinary traditions, no less than 11 complex flavours should be included in a meal: salty, sour, sweet, spicy, aromatic, nutty, pleasantly bitter, slightly bitter, astringent, full-bodied and light or clean tasting. Consistency, colour and fragrance are important for choosing the hand-mixed salad ingredients – lethok – that should also include seasonal wild herbs, edible flowers, shoots, young green or ripe fruits and vegetables, chillies, herbs and spices, seasoned with peanut oil.

Because of Myanmar's geographical position between two important gastronomic opposites, India and China and with more than 130 different ethnic minorities living in the country, the choice of produce seems to be more varied than in other Southeast Asian countries. Unusual salads are made with unique combinations, purloined from both neighbours as well as indigenous wild and cultivated ingredients.

Contact: The Strand Hotel, 92 Strand Road, Yangon, Myanmar
Telephone: +95 1243 377 Fax: + 95 1243 393
Email: info@thestrand.com.mm Web: www.ghmhotels.com

Gooseberry & okra salad with citron dressing

Serves 2

Ingredients
4 gooseberries, finely chopped
½ cucumber, peeled & seeds removed
2 tbs soy beansprouts
Inside of 2 stems of lemongrass, finely
  sliced
3 cherry tomatoes, chopped
3 shallots, finely sliced
1 small green chilli, deseeded & chopped
4 stems lemonbasil, leaves only
4 okra, or ladies fingers, sliced

Prepare the salad ingredients and mix
together with the dressing just before
serving.

Citron dressing
1 tbs peanut or any neutral tasting oil
1-2 tbs Burmese citron or lemon
½ tsp sea salt
½ tsp white pepper
1 tbs spring water

Mix the above together until well combined and set
aside for 30 minutes so that the flavours can develop.
Before serving, adjust the seasoning.

Oyster mushroom & chayote salad with pineapple dressing

Serves 2

Ingredients

2 small round aubergines, sliced & put into salty water for
   30 minutes to remove the bitterness. Drain & pat dry

3 cherry tomatoes, chopped

2 tbs kale or green cabbage leaves, chopped

4 winged beans or green beans, sliced

10 rosella or spinach leaves, shredded

100g oyster mushrooms, carefully cleaned & chopped

1 chayote, peeled & cut into small sticks

2 jengkol beans or soaked butter beans, sliced

6 onion chives with flowers, chopped

4 shallots, finely sliced

2 garlic cloves, chopped

1 sprig fresh curry leaf, leaves only

2 tbs fresh ripe mango, cubed

Pineapple dressing

3 tbs freshly made pineapple juice

1-2 tbs lime juice

1 tsp fresh ginger, chopped

2 small red chillies, deseeded & chopped

1-2 tsp palm sugar

½ tsp sea salt or to taste

Prepare the salad ingredients and set aside. Make the
dressing and adjust to taste. Carefully toss the dressing
with the salad before serving. Serve immediately.

Lentil salad

Serves 2

Ingredients

1 tbs split yellow lentils, soaked for
    24 hours until soft
1 tbs Burmese fermented lentils,
    washed and drained
4 stems peashoots, young leaves
    and tendrils only
4 shallots, finely sliced
2 garlic cloves, finely sliced
2 tbs young tamarind leaves
2 tbs cauliflower, sliced
2 baby bittergourd, finely sliced
2 fresh straw mushrooms, finely sliced
3 small red chilli, deseeded & chopped
5 green beans, sliced

Dressing

2 tbs palm sugar
4 tbs tamarind juice
1 tbs raw chickpea flour
1 tsp hot chilli powder
1 garlic clove, finely sliced
1 stalk coriander, leaves, stem
    and roots finely chopped
½ tsp sea salt

Prepare all the salad ingredients and set aside. Make the
dressing and adjust the flavour to your taste. Just before
serving mix the leaves and vegetables together and pour
over the dressing. Serve immediately.

Triple pickle salad

Serves 2

Ingredients
2 bunches pennywort or sentella, leaves only
4 shallots, finely sliced
3 garlic cloves, finely sliced
1 lg ripe, red tomato, chopped
1 green tomato, chopped
2 tbs soya beansprouts
2 small red chillies, deseeded and chopped
1 tbs yellow lentils, soaked for 24 hours then drained well
1 tbs fermented tea leaves (see *Tasty Extras*)
1 tbs pickled ginger
1 tbs pickled green mango
5 cm cats tongue pod, or mangetout peas, very finely
  sliced

Dressing
Juice of 2 limes
3 small thin green chillies, finely chopped
2 tbs palm sugar
¼ tsp sea salt or to taste

Prepare the ingredients for the salad. Make the dressing
and adjust the seasoning before adding to the salad just
before serving. Serve immediately at room temperature.

Young ginger salad

Serves 2

Ingredients

3 tbs young ginger, peeled and sliced

2 green tomatoes

1 tbs fermented white bamboo shoots, or bamboo
 shoots,sliced in fine slivers

1 tbs butter beans, soaked for 24 hours or more until
 sprouted & soft

3 tbs mint leaves, roughly chopped

4 shallots, finely sliced

10 young morning glory or water spinach leaves

1 *kinmon thi*, a small red Burmese gherkin or pickled
 cucumber with ¼ tsp sea salt and 1 tsp fresh orange juice

6 garlic chives with flowers

Dressing

2 tbs rice vinegar	3 tbs palm sugar
1 tsp raw chickpea flour	1 tbs mint, roughly chopped
1 shallot, chopped	1 tsp dried chilli, finely chopped
¼ tsp sea salt	

Mix all the above together and adjust the seasoning.
Prepare all the salad ingredients and mix carefully just
before adding the dressing. Serve immediately.

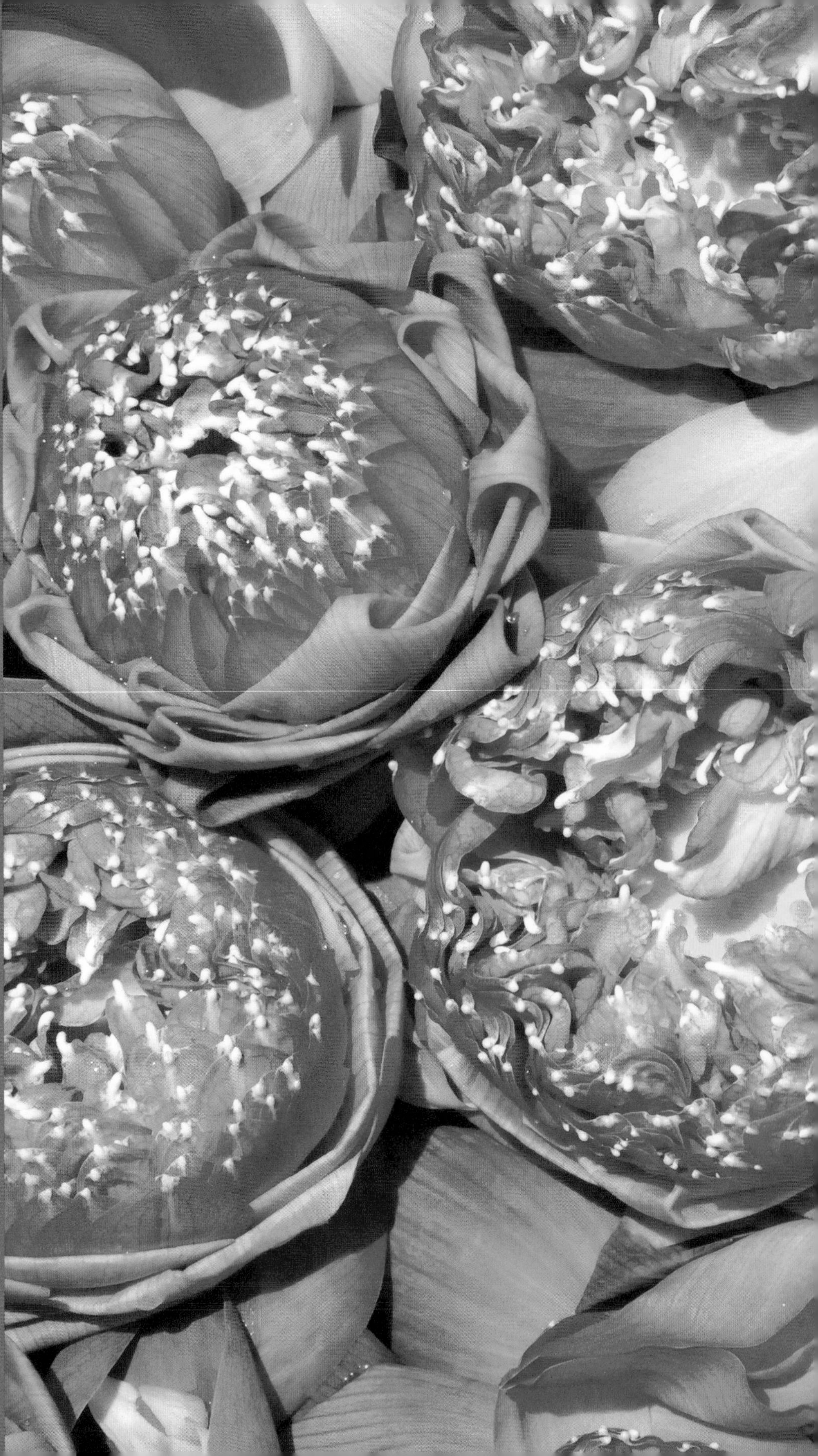

Appendices
Index

Appendices

Tasty Extras

Balinese Coconut & Spice Sprinkle Makes about 200g
1 fresh old coconut or 200g dried (unsweetened) coconut
Spice paste
4 garlic cloves, chopped
2 cm fresh turmeric, chopped
½ tsp fresh grated nutmeg
2 tbs crispy onions (*see below*)
2 tbs palm sugar, grated
½ tsp coriander seed
2 large red chilli, deseeded and chopped
4 small dried chillies, deseeded
2 tsp lime leaf, finely shredded
Grate the fresh coconut if using. Pound or blend the remaining ingredients together. Add to the coconut and dehydrate for approximately 12 hrs at 100 degrees. Check and turn over regularly.
How to keep: In a sealed sterilised jar in a cool dark place.
How to use: As a sprinkle or serve as a condiment.

Crispy Spiced Onions Makes about 200g
200g shallots, sliced finely and soaked in water with a pinch of salt for 20 minutes, drained well and dried for 20 minutes.
Spice paste
4 garlic cloves, chopped
1 tsp coriander seed
2 tbs palm sugar
2 cm turmeric, chopped
½ large red chilli, deseeded & chopped
1 tsp sea salt
Pound or blend all the above ingredients together apart from the shallots. Drain the shallots and dry well before adding the spice paste. Spread on sheets in the dehydrator and dry at 95 degrees for 15 hours, turning over regularly.
How to keep: In an airtight jar

Crispy Spiced Garlic Makes about 100g when dry
250g garlic cloves, finely sliced, soaked in salty water for 30 minutes then dried for 30 minutes.
Spice paste
3 cm kencur, chopped
4 cm kunyit, chopped
2 tbs palm sugar
½ tsp sea salt
Pound or blend the above together and adjust the seasoning to your taste. Add to the well dried garlic and dehydrate for 20-24 hours at 100 degrees or until crispy, turning over occasionally.
How to keep: In an airtight jar.
How to use: Sprinkle on absolutely everything or blend into spice pastes.

Asian-flavoured Spicy 'living' Nuts Makes about 450g
250g raw peanuts, skins left on
250g raw cashew nuts
Spice paste
1 tsp lime leaves, finely shredded
4 tbs palm sugar
½ tsp white peppercorns
1 tsp cumin
8 shallots, sliced
4 garlic cloves, sliced
2 cm turmeric, chopped
2 cm kencur, chopped
1 cm ginger, chopped
2 cm galangal, chopped
1 large red & green chilli, deseeded & chopped
1 small red chilli, deseeded & chopped
1 tsp sea salt or to taste
Pound or blend the spice paste ingredients together and adjust the seasoning. Spread on Teflex sheets in the dehydrator for an hour or two.
How to use: Serve as a snack or sprinkle, add to soups and salads.

Indonesian Crispy Potatoes Makes about 200g when dry
400g potatoes cut with the fine blade of the 'spiral' machine then soaked in salty water for 30 mins. Drain well and dry just before mixing with the spice paste.
Spice paste
3 cm turmeric, chopped
1tsp white peppercorns
2 garlic cloves, chopped
1 tsp sea salt
Pound or blend the above together, adjust the seasoning and mix with the well-drained potato 'noodles.' Dehydrate for about 20 hours at 100 degrees or until crispy, turning regularly.
How to keep: Use immediately or store only for a couple of days in an airtight container.
How to use: As a garnish for soups and salads.

'Rawfully Good' Sweet Chilli Sauce Makes 2 servings
4 large red chilli, finely chopped
2 small red chilli, finely chopped
3 or 4 tbs rice vinegar
3 tbs palm sugar
2 garlic cloves
½ tsp sea salt or to taste
Pound the above together but do and adjust the seasoning to make a fine sauce.
How to keep: Use immediately.
How to use: Add to soups & dressings or serve on the side as a condiment.

'Living' Sweet Soya Sauce For 2 servings

150 ml tamari or nama shoyu soy sauce
Pinch star aniseed powder
Pinch fresh nutmeg
1 tsp fresh ginger, grated
1 garlic clove, chopped
1 tsp Szechuan peppercorns
1-2 tbs palm sugar to taste

Pound or blend the above to make a smooth sauce. Adjust
the seasoning before serving.

How to keep: Make larger batches & store in sterilised bottles
in fridge.

How to use: As soy sauce.

Carrot & Coconut Crackers Makes about 8-10 crackers

100g fresh young coconut, cut into small strips
or 100g dried (unsweetened) coconut soaked in spring
water until soft, then squeezed well
100g carrots, grated or carrot pulp leftover from juicing

Spice paste

2 tbs raw peanuts, skins removed, soak 6 hours then dry well
2 tbs sweet soy sauce (*see below*)
1 tbs tamari
1 tsp palm sugar
1 tbs fresh lime juice

Pound or blend the above ingredients together and adjust
the seasoning before mixing in with the carrot and
coconut. Mix carefully and spread on Teflex sheets.
Dehydrate for 20-24 hours turning over once or twice, until
dry. Cut carefully into desired shapes with a plastic spatula
(so as not to damage the Teflex sheets) before the crackers
are completely dry.

How to keep: Store in an airtight container.

Burmese Pickled Tea Leaves For 2 servings

½ cup whole, good quality plain tea leaves or green tea
leaves or perfumed varieties like Earl Grey, lapsang
souchong or keemum
1 cup spring water
½ tsp sea salt
½ tsp sesame oil
1 small green chilli
Juice ½ lime
Palm sugar or to taste
1 tsp crispy garlic (*see above*)
1 tsp crispy nuts (*see above*)

Blend or pound the sesame oil, chilli, lime juice, salt &
palm sugar to make a paste. Adjust the seasonings to your
taste before adding the tea leaves. Pound again until the tea
leaves are part of the paste.

Use as sauce or dressing with vegetable 'rice' or serve as a
tasty dip.

After Juicing Green Crackers Makes about 15 crackers

250g vegetable pulp taken from the juicer after making
juice
150g each unsalted fresh cashews, sesame seeds, sunflower
seeds that have all been soaked separately for 6 hours.
Drain and dry

Spice paste

1 tbs large red chilli, deseeded & chopped
2-3 tbs good sesame oil
1 tsp cumin seed
2 tbs ginger, peeled & grated
2 garlic cloves, grated
Zest & juice of 1 lime
1 tbs galangal, chopped
1 tsp white pepper
Sea salt to taste

Remove the pulp from the juicer and keep in the fridge
until the nuts are ready to be added. After they have been
soaked and dried, blend them together with the vegetable
pulp. Blend or pound the spice paste ingredients together.
Add to the nut and vegetable mixture, adjust the seasoning
and and blend together until smooth. Spread thinly on the
Teflex sheets with a plastic spatula and dehydrate for
approximately 15 hours. Cut into desired shapes before
turning overhalf way through the drying process.

How to keep: When cool store in an airtight container. The
crackers can be crisped again in the deyhdrator for about 1
hour before using.

Ingredients

This list should help to provide readers with a list of some of the some of the many common and more unusual produce available all over SE-Asia. Further information and photographs of all the ingredients can be found online. Because so many of the following are available only in the region or occasionally at Asian grocers, experiment with flavours and buy produce available locally, wherever in the world this may be!

Agar Seaweed is a natural, calcium rich, vegan alternative to animal-based gelatine. Used all over Asia for cakes and desserts, agar is sold in small packets as flakes or powder and is easy to use.
How to use: Soak ½ tsp of powder or 3 tbs of flakes in 250 ml warm liquid for about 10 mins. It thickens only when cool, so set in fridge.
Warning: Agar may not set when combined with fresh papaya, mango or pineapple.
Buy: Asian grocers, health food shops or at Japanese grocers as *kanten*.
Substitute: None apart from gelatine.

Bee Products
Natural, unprocessed bee products contain most of the nutrients and anti-oxidants needed daily to boost the body's immune system. 'Beegans' are vegans who eat the bee products.

Bee Pollen is one of the most nutrient and amino acid rich, natural foods on the planet. Best eaten raw, the flavour can a little strange at first, so try adding a tablespoon of pollen into a juice or mixing a little water to make a cream to add to salad dressings. Store pollen in a cool, dark place, buy small amounts of best quality pollen and use quickly.
Buy: Health food shops or online.

Honey is the nectar made by bees from pollen they collect from fresh flowers. Raw honey is concentrated nectar that comes straight from the extractor and can contain particles of pollen or honeycomb. Raw, unfiltered honey has many nutrients and can be warmed but never heated.
Buy: Quality raw honey from health food shops, farmer's markets or online.
Substitute: Palm sugar.

Honeycombs are made from beeswax, produced from nectar gathered by bees. They can be eaten whole when fresh but the longer they are left, they become waxier and difficult to chew.
Buy: Health food shops, farmer's markets or online.
Substitute: Palm sugar.

Cocoa
Cocoa *lat. theobroma* or 'Food of the Gods' is not a fruit but a nut. Originating in South America, cacao is an 'superfood'

with more antioxidants than any other source and is one of the healthiest ingredients on the planet. Rich in minerals and a primary source for magnesium, cacao also has an high vitamin C content. Cocoa beans are full of chemicals that can induce a state of happiness and hightened awareness!

Cocoa Beans or Nibs are the seeds of the cacao fruit. These are fermented in the sun or dried at high temperatures to remove the outer shell and the mucus-like inner flesh. They have a rich, bitter chocolate flavour that can be addictive!
How to use: Eat a few whole beans each day. Grind or pound to add to or sprinkle on desserts and juices.
Buy: Try to source in a 'raw' state at health food shops or online.

Cocoa Butter is the natural fat that remains after processing the cocoa beans. It is creamy-white in colour, has very little taste, remains solid at room temperature and is a very versatile ingredient.
How to use: A good base for making 'living' sweets, cocoa butter can be grated and added to desserts or drinks. Store in airtight container in the fridge, (see *Bali, Puri Ganesha recipe*).
Buy: Health food shops or online. Shop around as prices can differ.

Cocoa Powder When the cocoa beans are pressed, two products, cocoa butter and cocoa solids result. The solids are pressed again resulting in a 'press cake' which is dried before processing into cocoa powder. Many of the commercial cocoa powders have been made using the 'Dutch' method to reduce the acidity of the beans and make the colour more attractive.
How to use: Add to or sprinkle on desserts, juices and drinks.
Buy: Health food shops or online.

Dairy Products
Although traditionally an essential part of Buddhist diets, dairy products have never been used in SE-Asian cuisine. If possible, try to reduce the consumption of dairy products or avoid them completely. Commercial milk and other dairy products are mucus-building and should ideally only be consumed occasionally. The modern mega dairy industry uses growth hormones, antibiotics and genetically modified feed which is automatically passed on to humans. For vegan alternatives, see *soy or nuts, pods & seeds*.

Edible Flowers
This is a list of flowers that can be eaten raw and covers only a few of the many hundreds of species to be found in different regions of SE-Asia. Flowers are used to add texture and colour to dishes, especially in Laos and Northern Thailand.
Buy: At the daily markets all over the region. Many companies offer Asian and European organically grown edible flowers on the internet. Source heirloom seeds and grow your own if you have a garden. The Allthingsnice

Spice Co. sells an extensive range of unusual products for 'Rawfully Good' food preparation. Hand-made in Bali, these are sourced in the wild or grown on small farms. For details and information contact: diana@puriganesha.net www.allthingsnicespicecompany.com

The following rules apply to edible or non-edible flowers to be found anywhere in the world:
• Use only wild or cultivated flowers that you know have been organically grown and not those bought from florists or garden centres, these have been sprayed with pesticides.
• Pick flowers in the early morning or evening when they have a much higher water content and remain fresh for longer.
• Use only perfect flower petals the same day and remove bitter stamens before use.
• Cut or tear off the lower white part of the petal because this can be bitter.
• Eat only flowers that you know are edible. If in doubt leave well alone! Some flowers are very poisonous!
• Don't use roadside flowers because of lead pollution from vehicles.
• Before using, wash the flowers carefully in water with an added tablespoon of salt or in diluted lemon juice to remove any insects. Leave to dry on a clean towel or pat dry with tissues.
• Many people can have allergic reactions to certain types of flowers, so use sparingly to begin with.
• The flowers of herbs and spices have a more intensive flavour than the leaves!

Acacia lat. *Acacia piñata*
Flowers used mainly in Thai soups and curries.
How to use: Pluck the flowers off the stems and sprinkle over salads.
Find: Growing wild.

Allium lat. *Allium*
This family covers more than 400 different species. Every part of these plants is edible and flavours range from mild and sweet to very strong. All allium flowers are tasty additions to soups and salads, dishes, especially chive and garlic flowers.
Buy: Grow your own or farmer's markets.

Asoka lat. *Saraca indica*
These beautiful multi-coloured yellow, orange and red flowers have a slightly sour taste.
How to use: Snip off the flowers, remove the stamens and add to soups and salads.
Find: In gardens or some markets in North Thailand and Laos.

Banana Flower lat. *Musa x paradisiacal*
Used in salads across the region.
How to use: Buy only smooth, unblemished flowers. Remove tough outer petals (use as serving containers) and small 'banana' stamens that grow between the inner petals. Chop and use only the softer, paler petals in the centre. Soak to

soften in water with added salt. Drain well and sprinkle with lime juice to prevent discolouration.
Buy: At markets across SE-Asia. Sometimes available at Asian grocers.

Bougainvillea lat. *Bougainvillaea hybrid*
The edible flowers of this climbing bush are found everywhere in SE-Asia. The flowers have little taste and the texture of older blooms is papery but once stamens are removed, single petals add colour to soups and salads.
Find: Ask for unsprayed cuttings from good garden centres. Bushes are easy to grow.

Butterfly Pea lat. *Clitoria ternatea*
This small blue flower comes from a creeper that grows wild in most SE-Asian countries. This natural blue colouring agent is used in Malaysian cuisine for rice dishes.
How to use: In large quantities, pea flowers have an intensive pea taste that must be carefully balanced with other flavours.
Buy: At some SE-Asian markets or growing wild all over the region.

Cabbage lat. *Brassica rapa*
The small yellow or white flowers can be used to decorate all kinds of 'raw' dishes.
How to use: Remove individual flowers and add to salads.
Buy: Chinese or Asian grocers.

Calendula lat. *Calendula officinalis*
Known as 'poor man's saffron', it has a mild saffron taste.
How to use: These decorative orange petals can be used fresh in salads or dried as a sprinkle.
Buy: Dried in health food shops in the West. Also easy to grow from seed, fresh flowers can sometimes be found in Indian supermarkets in the West and at Indonesian or Thai markets in SE-Asia. Ensure these have not been sprayed.

Coriander lat. *Coriandrum sativum*
These white flowers have the same intense flavour as the leaves. Can be used in soups and salads.
Buy: Source from herb growers or grow from seed.

Dill lat. *Anthum graveolens*
These yellow flowers taste more intense than the herb and give a special flavour to all kinds of dishes.
Buy: Source from herb growers or grow from seed.

Frangipani lat. *Plumeria family*
Many different colours and varieties of frangipani are found all over SE-Asia.
How to use: Remove the stamens and add single petals as a fragrant addition to soups and salads.
Buy: Fresh everyday at markets all over Bali or Java.
Substitute: Buy a cutting from a good garden supplier, place in pot with well-composted soil and keep in a warm place. These grow easily in the West if they are kept free of frost.

Gardenia lat. *Gardenia jasminnoides*

This fragrant flower can be used to decorate many dishes or added to soups and salads.
How to use: Single petals with the stamens removed.
Buy: Order unsprayed plants at good garden centres.

Gingerflower *lat. Zingiber officinale*
This waxy flower, in many shades of red and pink. Used for sambals and curries in Malaysia and Indonesia, it has a pleasantly astringent taste and adds a beautifully coloured 'crunch' sliced finely into to soups and salads.
How to use: Discard the outer petals, shred the inner ones very finely or pound into a paste with other ingredients.
Buy: Fresh at markets in Indonesia, Thailand or Malaysia and sometimes at Asian or Chinese grocers in the West.

Herb Flowers
Look for flowers of herbs and edible plants wherever you are. In Europe and N. America, angelica, borage, clover, dandelions, daisies, pansies, nasturtiums and many other edible herbs and flowers can be substituted for Asian flowers listed here. If in doubt, check online for lists of edible and poisonous flowers.

Hibiscus *lat. Hibiscus rosa-sinesnis*
Petals have an astringent fruity taste.
How to use: Remove stamens and use single petals as a garnish or soak for 10 mins in hot water to make a herbal tea.
Buy: Unsprayed plants at good garden centres or gardens all over SE-Asia.

Jasmine *lat. Jasminum sambac*
These highly scented flowers are used for jasmine tea, Vietnamese desserts or Javanese rice dishes.
How to use: Remove the stamens and lower green part from fresh flowers and add individual petals to salads or desserts.
How to make fresh jasmine water: Remove the stamens and soak the flowers (making sure that these have not been treated with pesticides) in water overnight. Drain, discard the flowers and put the water into a sterilized bottle.
Buy: Dried from Asian grocers or order unsprayed plants from good garden centres.

Jungle Geranium *lat. Ixora family*
Found in many different colours across the region.
How to use: Pluck single petals and remove the stamens. Add different coloured flowers to soups and salads.
Find: Easy to grow from seed or in gardens all over SE-Asia.

Kapok *lat. Ceiba pentandra*
These bright red flowers are added to many northern Thai dishes for their flavour and colour.
Buy: Village markets in North Thailand or growing wild throughout the region.

Lilly Flower *lat. Hemerocallis fulva*
The buds of dried lilly flowers have a special fragrance and are used in many Vietnamese dishes.
How to use: Soak in water with a little lime juice to soften.

Drain well before use.
Buy: Asian and Chinese grocers.

Lotus *lat. Nelumbo nucifera Gaertn.*
Usually pink, white or purple, this sacred flower is used for offerings all over Asia.
How to use: Every part of the plant is edible: seeds are eaten raw as a snack, young leaves and roots are chopped for salads.
Buy: Markets all over the region. Dried or fresh lotus seeds are available at Chinese grocers.

Marigold *lat. Tagetes patula*
Used for Buddhist and Hindu temple offerings.
How to use: Fresh or dried petals can be used as a decorative sprinkle.
Buy: Easy to grow from seed.

Neem *lat. Azadirachata indica*
Originated in India, has many medicinal uses. The trees grow wild all over the region. Cut off flower sprigs, soak in warm water for 20 mins before adding to soups and salads.
Buy: At markets in Thailand and Laos.

Pineapple Sage *lat. Saliva elegans*
The red tubular flowers and leaves have a distinct pineapple flavour. Indigenous to South America, this plant grows as a semi-weed across Europe and SE-Asia.
How to use: Add to salads and 'rice' dishes.
Buy: Specialist herb gardens or grow from seed.

Rose *lat. Rosa rugosa or R. gallica officinalis*
Roses are used in some parts of SE-Asia. Every rose is edible after removing the stamens.
How to use: Take the best petals for salads and deserts or freeze them in ice cube trays to add to drinks. Dry and use as a sprinkle but keep in a dark, dry place so that the colour and the fragrance do not disappear. Cut off the whitish base of each petal because this can be bitter.
Buy: Only unsprayed roses.

Rosella *lat. Hibiscus sabdariffa*
The dried calyx of the rosella plant are available all over the region. Soak in warm water to make an herbal tea or juice.
Buy: Dried at health food shops, specialist herbal tea suppliers or Asian grocers.

Spanish Flag *lat. Lantana camara*
A family of decorative weeds that grow all over the world.
How to use: Pluck off individual flowers, discard stamens, add to soups and salads.
Find: Growing wild everywhere.

Sunflower *lat. Helianthus*
Eat only young buds which have a flavour like artichokes. If already open, use petals to garnish soups and salads.
Find: Grow from seed.

Tamarind *lat. Tamarindus indica*

The tiny yellow flowers have a pungent, tamarind taste.
How to use: For garnishing soups and salads.
Find: Growing wild.

Tuberose *lat. Tuberosa*
Added to some Javanese rice dishes.
How to use: Remove the stamens and add the fragrant (the fragrance develops after dusk!) petals to salads and soups.
Buy: Order unsprayed stems from good florists.

Vegetable Hummingbird *lat. Sesbania grandiflora*
Widely used in many Javanese, Malaysian and Thai dishes.
How to use: Remove stamens of these decorative pink or white flowers before stuffing with vegetable pastes or using single petals in salads.
Buy: Javanese, Malaysian or Northern Thai markets.

Ylang-Ylang *lat. Cananga odorata*
One of the main offering flowers in Bali. Is used to perfume and decorate all over SE-Asia.
How to use: Remove the stamens, tear up single petals to add to soups or salads. Use sparingly because they have a very intense flavour.
Buy: Javanese and Balinese daily markets or order the plant from a specialist.

Zucchini *lat. Curcubito*
Flowers of the zucchini, squash and pumpkin family are all edible.
How to use: Wash carefully, trim off the stems and remove the stamens. Stuff with vegetable or nut purees or add to salads.
Buy: The flowers from organic farmers or super-markets.

Fruit

Eating copious amounts of fruit and drinking fruit juices can help to increase energy and lower the risk of cancer. Many fruits have a high fibre content, are cholesterol free and easily available.
Shopping & cleaning: Whether organically or commercially grown, the same rules for cleaning fruit apply as for vegetables (see *Vegetables*).
• Only buy fresh-looking blemish-free fruit with no bruising or mould.
• Small fruits and berries should be rinsed and drained well.
• Fruit should always be washed gently under running water, never use soap or detergent.
• After peeling fruit, wash it again, because some bacteria from the peel might still remain.
• Only peel and cut fresh fruit just before serving.
• Use one chopping board for fruit and another only for vegetables.

Ambarella *lat. Spondias dulcis*
Usually eaten raw, this green, crunchy fruit has an apple-mango taste and is well-known in Indonesia and Malaysia.
How to use: Shred raw and add to soups and salads.
Buy: Asian grocers or growing wild.

Apples *lat. Malus domestica*
Apples originated somewhere in the Caspian Sea region and many varieties grow in SE-Asia. Pectin in apples reduces cholesterol in the blood, they contain large amounts of anti-oxidants and the non-soluble fibre in the peel helps to move food through the body. Apples are easy to use for juices, salads, desserts and can be combined with all kinds of other fruit, vegetables and salad leaves for an extra healthy 'crunch'.
Tip: If possible, buy only organic or non-sprayed apples and wash the skin carefully, do not remove it! Always buy local instead of imported apples.

Avacados *lat. Persea americana*
Found in many parts of SE-Asia and full of anti-ageing potassium, vitamin E and amino acids, they are ideal for 'living' food creations. High in calories, so eat sparingly if you are on a diet. Used mostly in Indonesia and considered to be a fruit, avocados are usually juiced or sometimes added to spicy fruit salads.
Tip: Buy only semi-ripe fruit to use in salads but ripe fruit for soups and juices.

Banana *lat. Musaceae family*
These versatile plants grow in tropical and sub-tropical regions across the world. The hundreds of varieties can be divided into two main groups: sweet bananas for eating and starchy plantains that have to be cooked. Originating in Malaysia many thousands of years ago, banana plants have medicinal, culinary, packaging and decorative uses. Full of potassium, effective against stomach ulcers and are supposed to relieve depression! (see *Edible Flowers*).
Buy: Try some of the various kinds found in SE-Asian grocers.

Bael *lat. Aegle marmelos*
Can be eaten raw or bought dried in slices all over Laos and Thailand.
How to use: Soak slices in warm water to soften then chop finely or make a tea to help with eating disorders.
Buy: Dried at Thai or Asian grocers.

Coconuts *lat. Cocos nucifera*
Coconuts are one of the single most important daily staples and versatile ingredients used all over Asia.
How to choose and open old coconuts: Old coconuts should be heavy, have no mould around the 'eyes' and when shaken, have a great deal of juice inside. Pierce the eyes with a screwdriver to drain the water, strain to remove impurities and set aside. Pack the coconut in a towel, lay it on a hard surface and hit with a cleaver. Loosen the flesh from the shell and peel off the outer layer with a vegetable peeler.
How to make fresh coconut milk or cream: Grate the flesh and steep in hot water. Leave for 30 minutes then blend quickly. Strain through cheesecloth over a bowl and squeeze out any remaining liquid. Use the left over coconut to make 'living' crackers, sauces and dressings. Dry the flesh in the sun, oven or dehydrator and use in salads and desserts.
Subsitute: Buy small cartons of coconut cream and dilute as

required. Use quickly and store in fridge.

Choosing and opening young coconuts: Young coconuts should have a smooth green skin with only a few blemishes. Cut off the top, drain off the juice and scoop out the soft flesh. Cut this into slivers to make juices, soups and 'noodles' or add to the juice for a refreshing drink with ice and fresh lime juice.
Buy: At Asian grocers or buy fresh pieces of old coconuts or dried (unsweetened) grated coconut at supermarkets.

Cherimoya *lat. Annona squamosa*
A soft, sweet fruit with many black seeds originally from South America.
How to use: Eat raw or blend to make to juice.
Buy: Asian grocers and good supermarkets.

Cucumber Tree Fruit *lat. Averrhoa bilimbi*
A small, green fruit with a similar taste to starfruit. Gives a sour note to any dish.
How to use: Slice thinly before using and discard the seed.
Buy: Asian grocers.

Dragonfruit *lat. Helocereus undatus*
These white, yellow, or purple fruit with black seeds are members of the cactus family. Make colourful juices, sorbets and add to fruit salads.
How to use: Peel off decorative outer skin and slice into bite-size pieces.
Buy: Asian grocers and good supermarkets.

Dried Fruit is fruit which has been dried to remove moisture and lengthen the storage life.
How to use: To reconstitute dried fruit, soak it in fruit or citrus juice until soft. Dry fresh, 'organic' fruit in a dehydrator and also soak the slices in lemon juice before drying for 10 minutes to preserve more flavour. Eat raw, or chop and add to salads or puree for juices.
Buy: Commercial dried fruit has added sulfur dioxide so that the colour and taste remain more intense. Only buy untreated dried fruit from health food shops or good supermarkets and read the labels carefully.

Durian *lat. durio family*
Considered a delicacy in many SE-Asian countries, durians are adored by Asians but often hated by foreigners because of the obnoxious smell and texture. Often called 'the King of Fruits', durian has a smooth, buttery taste, and increases muscular fitness.
How to use: Eat raw make into an unusual sorbet. Break the fruit open and eat the segments.
Buy: Asian grocers.

Goji Berries *lat. Lycium barbarum*
These dried red 'superfood' berries originate in China. They have more beta carotene than carrots and more vitamin C than oranges. Full of antioxidants, amino acids and protein, eat 10-30g per day to strengthen the immune system.
How to use: Add this slightly sour and very versatile

ingredient to 'living' mueslis, salads or fruit salads.
Buy: Health food shops, good supermarkets and Chinese grocers.

Grapes are cultivated all over the region. Black varieties have a high mineral, antioxidant, vitamin and tannin content which helps to prevent and combat disease.
Tip: Try to buy 'organic' varieties that have not been sprayed with pesticides. If these are not available, remove as much pesticide residue as possible by washing grapes in a bowl of water with an added cup of distilled white vinegar. Rinse well with cold water.

Guava *lat. Myrtaceae family*
These fruits in many shapes and colours are to be found all over SE-Asia. Soft pink guavas are good for juice and the hard green ones can be sliced and served with a chilli sugar dip or added to salads.
How to use: Wash the skin and eat raw or slice before use.
Buy: Asian grocers and good supermarkets.

Hog Plum *lat. Spondias mombin*
Used mainly in Thailand and Laos, the small, yellow fruits have a sweet and sour flavour.
How to use: Add to salads or eat raw. Remove seed.
Buy: Asian grocers.

Jackfruit *lat. Artocarpus heterophyllus.*
This large, spiky fruit can be eaten raw as a snack or added to a salad.
How to use: Cut into pieces and remove the flesh between the segments. Discard the seeds.
Buy: Fresh from Asian grocers.

Kumquat *lat. Rutaceae family.*
Originally from China these small orange-like fruit now grow in much of SE-Asia.
How to use: Do not remove the skins after washing well. Slice into thin rounds and add to fruit or vegetable salads.
Buy: Chinese grocers and good supermarkets especially around the Chinese New Year period.

Langsat *lat. Lansium domesticum.*
Found in Indonesia, Malaysia and Thailand, these walnut-sized fruit have a thin brown skin and white fruit divided into segments.
How to use: Eat raw.
Buy: Asian grocers.

Lemon *lat. Citrus limon*
Lemons have been grown in China for thousands of years but although found all over SE-Asia, lime juice is preferred for most dishes.

Lime, Calamansi *lat. Calamansi X Citrofortunella microcarpa*
Native to the Philippines, the small lime with a green skin and orange flesh is used in Malaysian dishes. They have a

special, bitter orange taste.
How to use: Strain the juice and discard the fruit.
Buy: Philippino or Asian grocers.

Lime, Kaffir *lat. Citrus hystrix*
Every country in SE-Asia uses lime juice and the grated zest.
How to use: wash the peel well before grating and drying to
use as a garnish. Strain the juice.
Buy: Asian grocers and good supermarkets.

Limo *lat. Citrus aurantiifolia*
A tiny, bitter and intensely flavoured lime used mainly in
Balinese and Javanese dishes.
How to use: Cut into tiny pieces or add the juice.
Buy: Indonesian or Asian grocers.

Longan *lat. Euphoria longana*
Originally from China, longans have a smooth brown skin,
sweet glassy flesh and a small brown seed.
How to use: Eat raw or add to salads and desserts after
discarding the black seed.
Buy: Asian grocers and good supermarkets.

Lychee *lat. Litchi chinensi*
Cultivated in China for thousands of years, lychees are now
grown all over the region. Full of vitamin C, they have
knobbly pink skins and white perfumed flesh.
How to use: Peel the skin and discard the toxic brown seeds.
Buy: Asian grocers. Never buy tinned lychees, they have a
high sugar content.

Mango *lat. Mangifera indica*
This was the first variety of mango to be discovered near
the Burmese-Indian border. They have been cultivated
across the region since the 1st century AD and were taken
to South America by the Portugese in the 16th century.
Rich in vitamin C, vitamin A and carotenoids, hundreds of
varieties are grown in tropical climates all over the world.
How to use: Peel off the skin and cut carefully along the large
stone inside to remove the flesh.
Buy: Try different kinds from Asian grocers.

Mangosteen *lat. Garcinia mangostana*
This favourite tropical fruit probably originated in the
Indonesian Moluccan Islands but now grows all over SE-
Asia. The purple outer flesh contains a strong brown dye;
the inner white segments have a sweet, perfumed flavour.
Tip: Only buy small fruits that do not have a dry skin. Cut
open horizontally taking care not to cut through the actual
fruit segments. Discard the seeds.
Buy: Good supermarkets or Asian grocers.

Melon *lat. Cucurbitaceae family*
Many types of sweet melons grow all over SE-Asia. Most
common ones are the green-skinned white ones with pale
green flesh and little flavour, sweet honeydew melons and
different varieties of small or large red, yellow or white

watermelons.
Buy: Good supermarkets.

Noni *lat. Morinda citrifolia*
This alien-like, green fruit is one of Nature's 'superfoods'.
Rich in antioxidants, minerals and vitamins, noni juice is
used to treat depression and insomnia.
How to use: The taste of the ripe fruit is over-powering,
reminiscent of blue cheese, so combine with other fruits to
make one of the best and most healthy juices on the planet!
Buy: Fresh from Asian grocers or in liquid form from health
food stores. Be sure to check the label.

Papaya *lat. Carica papaya*
This healing fruit grows profusely all over SE-Asia. The ripe
fruit has stomach-soothing and gas-eliminating properties.
See also Nuts & Seeds.
How to use: Young, green papayas are grated for salads especially in Thailand and Laos. Ripe papayas are eaten raw or
added to fruit salads.
Buy: Unblemished fruit from Asian grocers or good
supermarkets.

Passionfruit *lat. Passiflora edulis*
Also known as *granadilla* and imported originally from
Middle and South America, two varieties grow in SE-Asia,
the small brown and the larger orange ones.
How to use: Open carefully, strain away the seeds and discard
if you dislike the crunch. Use for juice, soups and salads.
Buy: Good supermarkets or Asian grocers.

Persimmon or Kaki *lat. Diospyros kaki*
Originating in Japan, they grow all over the region. Can
only be eaten when overripe. Full of vitamin A and beta-
carotene.
How to use: Peel if the skin is too thick. Use for salads and
desserts.
Buy: Good supermarkets and Asian grocers.

Pineapple *lat. Ananas comosus*
Pineappels came to SE-Asia from India. Being alkaline, they
combat acidity in the body.
Note: Smooth-leaf pineapples may be larger and juicier but
rough-leaf pineapples are sweeter.
Buy: Asian grocers or good supermarkets.

Pomegranate *lat. Punica granatum*
Wild all over the region, the seeds are both decorative and
healthy being a good source of antioxidants and enzymes.
How to use: Rub on a hard surface to loosen the seeds. Break
open, remove seeds from the yellow pith and add to salads
or fruit salads.
Buy: Dark red pomegranates at supermarkets, Asian or Arabic
grocers.

Pomelo *lat. Citrus grandis*
This giant pale yellow-fleshed member of the grapefruit

family is available all over the region.

How to use: Peel off the outer skin and thick pith. Remove the segments from the membranes, flake the flesh to eat as a snack or use in salads.

Buy: Asian grocers.

Substitute: Any other type of grapefruit.

Rambutan *lat. Nephelium lappaceum*

Probably originatin in Malaysia, the pink skin is covered in soft, hairy spikes. The opaque fruit is sweet and juicy. Make into sorbets and add to fruit salads.

How to use: Peel off the outer skin and discard seed.

Buy: Good supermarkets and Asian grocers.

Roseapple or Waterapple *lat. Syzygium jambos*

These crunchy, thirst-quenching fruit have a slight rose flavour and are used throughout SE Asia in spicy fruit salads.

How to use: Eat raw or add to salads, discarding core and seeds.

Buy: Asian grocers.

Sapodilla *lat. Manilkara zapota*

A native Mexican fruit found all over SE-Asia, it can only be eaten when very ripe and has a wonderfully sweet taste.

How to use: Peel off the skin and eat raw or cut into slices.

Buy: Asian grocers.

Snakefruit *lat. Salacca zalacca*

This small fruit native to Malaysia and Indonesia, has a snake-like skin and firm, creamy flesh.

How to use: Peel off skin. Eat raw or chop the flesh to add to salads and fruit salads. Discard seeds.

Buy: Only fresh-looking fruits from Asian grocers.

Soursop *lat. Guanabanus muricatus*

Originally from Mexico this is a large, prickly green fruit with fragrant soft white flesh.

How to use: Cut open and remove the creamy flesh. Discard seeds and use to make sorbets or juices.

Buy: Asian grocers.

Starapple *lat. Chrysophyllum cainito*

Found all over Java, Thailand and Laos, the fruit has a shiny green or purple skin and a milky sap appears when cut. The gel-like flesh is very sweet!

How to use: Peel off the thin skin, discard the seeds and slice. Eat raw or use in fruit salads.

Buy: Markets in North Thailand, Indonesia and Laos or Asian grocers.

Starfruit or Carambola *lat. carambola*

This sour, yellow fruit indigenous to the region, is one of the main ingredients used in the sweet, sour and spicy salads enjoyed in Thailand and Indonesia.

How to use: Cut into thin slices and discard seeds.

Buy: Good supermarkets and Asian grocers.

Stargooseberry *lat. phyllanthus acidus*

Grows all over the region and is used in Burmese recipes.

How to use: Slice very thinly and use sparingly because they are very sour indeed!

Buy: Burmese or Asian grocers.

Substitute: Gooseberries.

Strawberry *lat. fragaria family*

Originally a wild berry from the East coast of Canada, they are now cash crops in many SE-Asian countries. They contain large amounts of vitamin C and are very versatile.

Buy: Commercially-grown strawberries are usually sprayed with pesticides. Try sourcing only seasonal 'organic' ones or wash very well!

Tamarillo *lat. solanum betaceum*

The small, egg-shaped fruit with orange flesh, black seeds and a bitter-sweet taste are found across the region.

How to use: Peel off the thin skin, discard the seeds and slice. Use ripe fruit in desserts or sorbets.

Buy: Asian grocers and good supermarkets.

Tangerine *lat. citrus reticulata*

Originating in China these are used in Chinese medicine to aid digestion problems. There are many different varieties, but those found in the region are small, have many pips and the aroma is usually better than the flavour.

Buy: Asian or Chinese grocers.

Substitute: Satsumas or clementines in the West.

Herbs & Edible Leaves

Many different kinds of wild and cultivated herbs and leaves are used raw in recipes all over the region, especially in the northern provinces of Malaysia, Thailand and Laos. Some of the ingredients listed can be found in other parts of the world, but substitute any wild or cultivated alternatives. Source unusual herbs and edible leaves from local farms, order from heirloom seed suppliers and grow from seed. An invaluable website for sourcing the names of herbs and spices in up to 64 different languages is *Gernot Katzer's Spice Pages:* www.unigraz.at/~katzer/engl/index.html

Tips for storing herbs & leaves:

• Always take a cooler bag when shopping for salads or fresh leaves because bacteria begins to grow when produce reaches a temperature of more than 8 degrees.

• If possible, always buy the freshest herbs and leaves that have no blemishes or insect holes.

• Dip fresh herbs and leaves in spring water with some added salt to remove any insects or larvae.

• Use as quickly as possible so that the nutrients and flavours are retained.

• Buy only as required.

• Spray unwashed, fresh leaves and herbs with spring water, wrap carefully in paper towels, put into plastic bags and store in the fridge.

• Alternatively, cut 1 cm off the stems, stand the herbs or leaves in cold water and cover with a plastic bag, store in the fridge and use quickly.

• If Asian herbs are sold with roots, cut them off and stand in spring water, changing it every two days. If more roots develop after a week, they can be planted in a pot. This is not always successful at first, so keep trying!

• Tearing or chopping herbs releases their essential oils, so never do this in advance, always just before serving.

• Darker the leaves, higher the nutrient content.

• If using dried herbs, these should be added at the beginning of the recipe.

• Remove and discard the outer leaves of any kind of greens before rinsing well.

• If the herb plants have flowers, they are in their reproductive cycle so the leaves and stems will not be as tasty as usual – just use the flowers!

• If you can only buy salad in bags, check the packing date carefully and do not buy if the salad is at all discoloured or if there is brown liquid at the bottom of bag.

• Always buy and eat bag salad the same day and never put a bag that has been opened bag back in the fridge to re-use.

• Many 'bagged' salads are treated with CO_2 to stop further growth. Wash well to remove as much residue as possible.

Acacia *lat. Acacia piñata*
The tasty pods and young leaves are used in Malaysian and Thai dishes.
How to use: Strip young leaves off the stems and add to soups and salads.
Find: Growing wild.

Agathi *lat. Sesbania grandiflora*
The leaves have a similar appearance to tamarind and young shoots can be used in soups and salads.
How to use: Remove the leaves and discard the stems. Every part of the tree is used for medicinal purposes.
Find: Growing wild.

Aloe Vera *lat. Aloe vera*
This succulent, healing plant grows all over Asia, the Middle East and southern Mediterranean.
How to use: Slice the fleshy leaves horizontally, scrape out the gel and add to sauces and dressings. The gel is bitter, so balance the flavour with other ingredients.
Buy: Buy single leaves from Thai or Asian grocers. Buy from good garden centres or grow in pots from cuttings.

Amaranth *lat. Amaranthus spinosus*
Known as 'Asian spinach', it grows wild and can be found at markets all over SE-Asia, (see *Vegetables*).
How to use: Add whole young leaves to soups and curries or shred older leaves.
Substitute: Any kind of spinach.

Basil *lat. Ocimum family*
There are more than 150 varieties of basil throughout the world. Originally from India, Hindus regard it as a holy plant. The following three are used throughout SE-Asia:

Basil, Holy *lat. Ocimum sanctum*
Used throughout SE-Asia, especially Thailand and Vietnam.

How to use: Tear the leaves and add just before serving.
Buy: Asian grocers or good supermarkets.

Basil, Lemon *lat. Ocimum cirtiodorum*
Used as an ingredient for raw vegetable salads, *sambals* and sauces in Indonesia and Thailand.
How to use: (see *above*).
Buy: Asian grocers or grow in pots from seed.

Basil, Sweet *lat. Ocimum basilicum*
This fragrant addition to any dish is used extensively in Thailand, Malaysia, Java and Vietnam.
How to use: (see *above*).
Buy: (see *above*).

Betel *lat. Piper*
Has been used with other ingredients as a mild relaxant in the region for hundreds of years.
How to use: Shred finely before use. Fresh young leaves add a bitter note to soups or salads.
Buy: Asian grocers.

Bok Choy A member of the *brassica* cabbage family.
How to use: Baby bok choy can be used whole. Just trim off the bottom of the stems. Chop or shred the white stalks and green leaves of large bok choy for use in salads.
Buy: Asian grocers or good supermarkets.

Cashew *lat. Anacardium occidentale*
Young leaves have a slight cashew taste and are shredded for Malaysian *ulam* salads.
Find: Growing wild.

Cassava *lat. Manihot esculenta*
A good source of vitamin A, these leaves help to combat anemia and protein deficiencies.
How to use: Shred young leaves for salads or soups.
Find: Growing wild all over Asia. Asian grocers.

Chinese Celery *lat. Apium gravolens*
Not at all similar to the mild European celery, the intensely flavoured leaves are used mainly in Indonesia and Malaysia.
How to use: Chop finely and use sparingly in soups and salads.
Substitute: European celery.

Chinese Leaves *lat. Brassica rapa subsp. Pekinensis*
This versatile long-leafed, white sweet cabbage is grown all over the region.
How to use: Discard the outer leaves then shred or chop to use in salads and soups.
Buy: Good supermarkets or Asian grocers.

Chrysanthemum *lat. Chrysanthemum coronarium var. spatiosum*
Not to be confused with chrysanthemum varieties found in the West.
How to use: Young leaves are used in Thai and Vietnamese dishes and can be added to soups and salads.
Find: Asian grocers or grow from seed.

Coriander *lat. Coriandrum sativum*
One of the most widely used herbs in SE-Asia. Either loved or hated by many people, it helps eliminate toxic heavy metals from the body.
How to use the roots: Clean well and remove the small side roots. Chop and pound or blend to a smooth paste to add to dressings, soups and sauces.
Buy: Buy with the roots from Asian grocers or good supermarkets.

Cosmos *lat. Cosmos caudatus*
These young leaves are a favourite Malaysian *ulam* ingredient and delicious in soups and salads.
Find: Growing wild or grow from seed.

Curry *lat. Murrya koenigii*
One of the single most important ingredients in Malaysian cuisine, but rarely used in other parts of SE-Asia. The leaves have a pungent taste with aniseed overtones.
Tip: Strip the leaves from the stems, chop or use whole. Always buy fresh leaves and store for no more than a day in the fridge because they loose their flavour very quickly. Never buy dried leaves because these have no taste at all.
Buy: Asian grocers.

Daun Suji *lat. Pleomele angustifolia*
Used extensively in Indonesia as a natural sweet tasting green food colouring.
How to use: Shred the leaves for salads or dry and powder for colouring.
Find: Growing wild.

Dill *lat. Anethum graveolens*
Probably brought to SE-Asia by the French during colonial times, dill is used extensively in Laos and Vietnam.
Buy: Supermarkets or grow from seed.

Drumstick *lat. Moringa olifera*
This 'superfood' tree grows all over the region. The leaves are made into a soup in everyday Malaysian and Indonesian cuisine. Rich in Vitamin A, iron and many other minerals, young leaves can be added to soups and salads.
How to use: Remove leaves from stems before using.
Find: Growing wild.

Fern *lat. Dryopteris erythrosora*
Used extensively in Indonesian and Malaysian cuisine.
How to use: Chop off just the tips and young leaves.
Buy: Asian grocers.

Garlic Chives *lat. Allium tuberosum*
The flat, garlic-tasting leaves are used in Vietnamese dishes.
How to use: Shred finely for soups, salads or as a garnish.
Buy: Asian grocers or grow from seed.

Goji *lat. Lyceum chinense*
Beware of the many thorns on the stems of these 'superfood' gojiberry plants. The leaves and berries have

always been an important ingredient in Chinese medicine.
How to use: Use whole young leaves or shred finely.
Find: Chinese grocers of health food shops.

Hibiscus family Leaves are used for herbal teas or shredded finely to be added to *ulam* dishes in Malaysia.
How to use: Shred the youngest most tender leaves.
Find: Growing wild or in gardens.

Katuk *lat. Sanropus androgynus*
Found in Indonesia and Malaysia, the new leaves and pink flowers are shredded and used in salads.
Find: Growing wild.

Kencur *lat. Kaempferia galanga*
Confusion reigns about the name so I keep to the original Indonesian one. Aromatic young leaves are finely shredded before adding to soups and salads, (see *Spices*).
Tip: Only buy fresh kencur and because it is difficult to find, buy more and try to plant in a pot in a warm spot with good, well-watered soil.
Buy: Indonesian or Asian grocers.

Laksa Leaf or Vietnamese Mint *lat. Polygonum odoratum*
The most important ingredient in Malaysian *laksa* and many Vietnamese dishes. Its very specific taste has no substitute.
How to use: Shred or add whole leaves to raw dishes. After the stems have been cut the flavour disappears quickly.
Buy: Asian grocers.

Lemongrass *lat. Cymbopogon citratus*
The fragrant grass is used extensively all over SE-Asia. Only buy fresh, pliable stems. Store in a plastic bag in the fridge and use quickly.
How to use: Remove the outer, woody leaves until you reach the inner, soft stem. Chop this finely and add to sauces, dressings, soups and teas, blend or pound together with other spices to make pastes.
Tip: Never buy dry or powdered products as these have little or no flavour. In the West, buy the freshest stems of lemongrass, plant in good soil in a sunny corner of the garden.
Buy: Good supermarkets or Asian grocers.

Lettuce *lat. Lactuca sativa*
Many varieties of traditional and new, imported species are cultivated all over SE-Asia. Originating in the Mediterranean thousands of years ago, today the three main varieties grown in SE-Asia are butterhead, crisphead and romaine.
Buy: Try to buy only 'organically' grown lettuce.

Lettuce, Sea *lat. Ulva lactua*
A traditional Vietnamese favourite, available dried or fresh.
How to use: Soak dried lettuce until soft and shred before use. Add sparingly to soups and salads.
Buy: Fresh or dried at Vietnamese grocers.

Lime Leaves, Kaffir *lat. Citrus hysterix*
These smooth green leaves grow in pairs and are added

whole or finely shredded to many dishes all over the region, especially in Thailand and Indonesia.
How to use: Remove the middle woody part of the leaf and shred very finely to add to soups, salads or spice pastes.
Tip: Wash and store fresh leaves in the freezer to keep the essential oils from evaporating.
Buy: Frozen are better than dried but fresh ones are available at Asian grocers or supermarkets.

Melinjo lat. Gnetum gnemon
The tree grows all over the region. Young leaves are only eaten in Indonesia where the small orange and green fruit are eaten raw or made into crackers.
Buy: Sometimes available at Asian grocers.

Mint lat. Mentha family
There are nearly 1,000 varieties of mint throughout the world. Source more interesting flavoured plants or varieties with more flowers, or grow from seed.
How to use: Shred the leaves finely or tear into pieces and add to soups, salads, teas or dressings.
Buy: From Asian grocers or good supermarkets.

Peppermint Mentha x piperita
A variety of mint used in Lao, Thai and Vietnamese dishes.
Buy: Supermarkets and Asian grocers.

Spearmint lat. Mentha spicata
A strong plant used mainly in Thai and Vietnamese dishes.
Buy: Arabic or Asian grocers, good supermarkets.

Noni or Morinda lat. Morinda citrifolia
leaves of the 'superfood' noni fruit.
How to use: Shred young leaves to add to soups and salads.
Find: Growing wild.
Substitute: A few drops of noni juice available from health food shops.

Pandanus Leaf or Screwpine lat. Pandanus odoratissimus
These long, thin green leaves are used all over Asia to colour or flavour sweets and desserts, as well as for decorations and offering containers for religious rituals.
How to use: Shred the leaves very finely before using sparingly, as the taste is intense.
Buy: If the fresh leaves are unavailable, try pandan essence found in most Asian or Indian grocers.

Pennywort lat. Centella asiatica
This soft green leaf, used for Malaysian ulams and kerabus, is also popular in Vietnam and Laos.
How to use: Snip off whole leaves to use in soups or salads.
Find: At SE-Asian markets, or grow from seed.

Pepper lat. Piper sarmentosum
The leaves are used in Thailand and Vietnam to wrap the traditional miang dishes and in Malaysia as one of the shedded leaves for nasi ulam.

How to use: Shred the freshest possible leaves before using.
Buy: Asian grocers.

Pondweed, Oval-leaved lat. Monochoria vaginalis
Used in Malaysian ulams, crunchy and full of nutrients, this weed grows wild in paddy fields all over the region.
How to use: Finely chop young leaves and fleshy stems.
Find: Growing wild or at daily markets in SE-Asia.
Substitute: Spinach or morning glory.

Pumpkin lat. Cucubita family
Found across the region.
How to use: Chop young leaves, shoots and tendrils.
Find: In gardens or from market gardeners.

Rice Paddy Herb lat. Limnophila chinensis var. aromatica
Used in Northern Thai, Lao and in Vietnamese dishes, it has an unusual lemon and cumin flavour.
How to use: Use only the leaves, discard the stems.
Buy: Asian or Vietnamese grocers.

Salam Leaf lat. Syzygium polyantha
Used mainly in Indonesian dishes. The dried leaves only release their flavour when cooked or soaked in water.
How to use: Fresh leaves can be finely chopped to add to salads. The flavour is a little like a bay leaf.
Buy: Indonesian grocers.

Sawtooth Coriander lat. Eryngium foetidum
The leaves have a milder taste than coriander and are used all over the region.
How to use: Shred the long leaves and add to salads or soups.
Buy: Asian grocers.
Substitute: Coriander leaves.

Shizo lat. Perilla frutescens
The red or green leaves are used in Thai and Vietnamese dishes.
How to use: Shred finely, tear into pieces or use small ones whole in salads or for decoration.
Buy: Japanese or Vietnamese grocers.

Tamarind lat. Tamarindus indica
The young shoots have a pleasant astringent taste.
How to use: Use only young leaves in soups and salads.
Find: Growing wild.
Substitute: Add tamarind paste to sauces or dressings.

Turmeric lat. Curcuma
Used in ulams in Malaysia, the long, fresh leaves are very tasty and give an intense flavour to salads and soups. It is anti-inflammatory and antiseptic.
Tip: Buy some really fresh turmeric from an Asian grocer, put it in a pot with good, well-watered soil and stand in a warm, sunny place.
How to use: Finely shred a handful of these large leaves and add to soups and salads.
Buy: Asian grocers or good supermarkets.

Watercress *lat. Nasturtium officinale*
Available across the region, the young shoots and leaves are full of vitamin C and many antioxidants.
How to use: Chop the leaves with the stems or just use the leaves. Discard any discoloured leaves.
Buy: Good supermarkets.

Water Dropwort *lat. Oenanthe javanica*
Used mainly in Malaysian dishes, the leaves loose their flavour very quickly.
How to use: Finely shred the leaves or use young ones whole.
Find: Growing wild, or Javanese markets.

Waterspinach or Morning Glory *lat. Ipomoea aquatica*
Different varieties are available across the region. The plant has hollow stems and triangular leaves.
How to use: Keep young leaves whole and finely chop the stems to add to soups and salads.
Buy: Asian grocers.

Nuts Pods & Seeds
A wealth of nutrients, vitamins and minerals are packed into all the different varieties of nuts and seeds. To make them more digestible for 'living' food, they should be soaked for between 1-12 hours. Although high in calories, the long list of health-giving properties is impressive.
• Not one of the nuts and seeds available in the West is actually 'raw'. To ensure a longer shelf life, they have all been treated with the propylene dioxide or pasteurized at high temperatures. Even those labelled 'organic' or 'raw' will have been pasteurized.
• If using nuts for 'living' food, never buy them already salted or roasted.
• It is always better to buy unprocessed nuts in the shell.
• Always check packing dates carefully.
• Buy nuts from health food shops or good supermarkets.
• Nuts that have been pasteurized cannot be sprouted.

Annato Seeds *lat. Bixa orellana*
Used as a natural red colouring agent.
How to use: Grind to a powder and add to dishes as required.
Buy: Chinese grocers.
Substitute: Organic, vegan food colouring.

Candlenuts *lat. Aleurites moluccana* These nuts are used in Malaysian and Indonesian cuisine as a thickening agent but are poisonous if used raw in large quantities.
How to use: Chop finely then pound and add to spice pastes.
Substitute: None.

Cashews *lat. Anacardium occidentale*
The shells are toxic, so all the 'raw' cashews available in health food shops have been pasteurized at high temperatures after shelling. They have a high carbohydrate and magnesium content. Always buy unsalted cashews to use in 'living' food dishes.
How to use: Do not store for too long. If they taste or smell rancid, throw away.

Buy: Health food shops or good supermarkets.

Jenkol Beans *lat. Archidendron jiringa*
Young bean pods are sliced, chopped or eaten raw as a favourite seasonal ingredient, especially in Java and Malaysia.
Buy: Indonesian or Malaysian grocers.

Papaya Seeds *lat. Carica papaya*
When using fresh papaya, do not discard the seeds.
How to use: If the seeds are still fresh, crush and add to salads. Alternatively, dry or dehydrate, then grind coarsely and use as a healthy sprinkle and crunch for all dishes.

Peanuts *lat. Arachis hypogaea*
Originally brought by Portugese traders from South America, they have become a staple all over SE-Asia.
Tip: Always buy 'raw' peanuts with the skins still intact for added nutritional value. Ensure that the nuts do not have any mould as this can be toxic.
Buy: Health food shops or Asian grocers.

Pumpkin Seeds *lat. Curcurbita pepo*
Rich in protein and minerals and readily available. Mix with other seeds and add to salads.
Buy: Health food shops or Asian grocers.

Sesame Seeds *lat. Sesamum indicum*
These, tiny black and white seeds are grown all over the world. The seeds are rich in minerals and calcium.
How to use: As a sprinkle or grind into a paste to add to sauces and dressings.
Buy: Health food shops, Asian grocers or good supermarkets.

Stinkbeans *lat. Parkia speciosa*
Especially popular in Indonesia and Malaysia.
How to use: Take out of the pods, chop or leave whole. They have a very intensive garlic taste.
Buy: Asian and Chinese grocers.

Sunflower Seeds *lat. Helianthus*
A rich source of magnesium, protein and vitamins, they help to lower cholesterol levels.
How to use: Add to salads or soups.
Buy: Health food shops and supermarkets.

Tamarind *lat. Tamarindus indica*
The pods are lined with seeds and a tart-tasting pulp used in many dishes throughout the region. This can be chopped finely and added to soups and salads.
How to use: Buy a block of tamarind pulp, cut off a piece and soak in hot water. Discard seeds. Use the resulting brown water to flavour soups and sauces.
Buy: For the tastiest results, buy only as a block of pulp with the seeds at Asian or Indian grocers. Sometimes fresh pink and green tamarind is available at Thai markets.

Oils & Vinegars

Tips for storing and using oils:
• Always use virgin, cold-pressed oils within 6 months of opening.
• Never use oils that smell or taste at all rancid.
• Buy in small quantites as needed.
• If no cold-pressed Asian oils i.e. peanut or coconut are available, always use extra virgin olive oil, adding more Asian herbs and spices to offset the taste.
• Try to limit the use of commercial salad or cooking oils altogether. These have been over refined with the use of solvents, even nickel as a metal catalyst, bleached and hydrogenated. Various studies show that these oils could be an important factor in the development of some cancers.
• Always read the labels very carefully.
Buy: Source good oils at Asian grocers, health food shops, on line.

Avocado Oil
Has as many healthy, unsaturated fats as virgin olive oil.
Buy: Only cold-pressed virgin oil from health food shops, good supermarkets or online.

Coconut Oil
Virgin coconut oil is a 'superfood', known to enhance the body's metabolism, boost the immune system and help combat degenerative diseases. Used as an essential cooking ingredient in Asia for thousands of years, its positive medicinal properties are unchallenged. If you like the taste, add a teaspoon to soups, dressings and sauces.
Buy: Only cold-pressed virgin coconut oil from Asian grocers or the internet and always check the labels.

Food Grade A Organic Essential Oils
The ancient Egyptians distilled essential oils from plants more than 5,000 years ago to make perfume. Today organic Grade A oils are available to the food industry. They are more than 50 times more potent than the plants they are distilled from and some have very special therapeutic properties. Great care is needed when buying, sourcing and using the tiny amounts needed to flavour dishes.
Buy: Only certified organic food grade A oils from reputable suppliers.

Olive Oil
The best olive oils have to include 'cold-pressed' and 'unfiltered' on the label. It can be used for Asian food if the flavours are adjusted accordingly.
Buy: Buy small bottles from different suppliers until you find one that you prefer to use.

Palm Oil lat *Elaeis guineensis*
Cold-pressed red palm oil has nearly the same health properties as cold-pressed coconut oil and can be used in the same way.
Buy: Asian grocers or good supermarkets.

Peanut Oil
Peanuts for oil production are usually heavily sprayed and 'organic' peanut oil is not readily available.
Buy: Try health food shops or online.

Sesame or Teel Oil
Used as a flavour enhancer in SE-Asia, the oils are not used for cooking but added just before serving. They are made from pressed, roasted sesame seeds. The cold-pressed 'virgin' sesame oil available in health food shops is 'raw' but has little or no flavour.
Tip: Buy small bottles of the best oil available. Once opened, use quickly.
Buy: Asian or Japanese grocers.

Soybean Oil
High in polyunsaturated and natural Omega-3 fats it is known to reduce cholesterol. Read the label carefully to make sure that the oil is not made from GMO soybeans.
Buy: Good supermarkets and Asian grocers.

Vinegar
All rice wine vinegars used in Asian cuisine come from fermented rice or the residues of alcoholic rice wine production. Many Asian vinegars such as Mirin have different amounts of sugar and salt added. Source natural, unpasteurized and unfiltered vinegar.
Buy: Health food shops, internet.

Rice & Rice Products
Rice is a staple for about 60% of the world's population. Cultivated for thousands of years, there are approx. 8,000 different strains grown around the world. Rice is gluten free and easily digestible. It naturally absorbs and balances strong flavours. Experiment and prepare unusual combinations using cooked natural brown, red or black rice, shredded 'living' herbs, leaves, vegetables and tasty sauces and dressings (see *Malaysia* for ideas).
Buy: Natural brown (unhulled) rice for sprouting from health food shops and red or black SE-Asian rice from Asian grocers. Wash and rinse well a few times before using. Discard the rinsing water.

Rice Papers
The thin spring roll papers made with rice flour and water have a rattan pattern, the hallmark of traditional papers.
How to use: Dip each one in water. Place on clean dry cloth before use.
Buy: Source different shapes and sizes at Asian and Vietnamese grocers.

Sea Vegetables or Seaweeds
Sea Vegetables or Seaweeds are probably the most nutrient dense foods on the planet, containing more than twenty times the minerals contained in other edible leaves and herbs. They boost the immune system and help to correct imbalances in the body caused by a modern diet.
How to use: Soak for 5-10 mins before using, drain well.

Chop finely before adding to salads or soups.
Note: Most sea vegetable products have been dried at high temperatures, even when 'raw' is included on the label.
Buy: Fresh sea vegetables are available at markets in SE-Asia. Dried varieties can be found in Japanese supermarkets.

Soy Products

Soy Products are used extensively in 'living' food cuisine, atthough the soy beans are boiled before any of the products are made. Many of these products contain genetically modified beans imported from the USA. Today many farmers throughout the region are reverting to making soy products using local non-GMO soy beans.

Miso

A fermented soy, grain or rice paste used for flavouring soups and dressings. Commercial miso can have a high salt content and added sugar so check the labels, buy the best and use sparingly.

Nama Shoyu

This naturally fermented, unpasteurised soy sauce has equal amounts of soy beans, wheat and less salt than other sauces.
Buy: Japanese grocers and good supermarkets. Check the labels for additives.

Soy Beans

lat. Glycine max Originally from China, these beans have been used as a nutrient rich food source for thousands of years and should be the base for all soy products.

Soy Milk

Soy milk is pressed from boiled soy beans and used for making tofu. Although not 'raw' it is a non-dairy, vegan alternative and has more protein than cow's milk.
Tip: Soy milk curdles if mixed with lime or lemon juice.
Buy: Good supermarkets. Always check the dates on the packaging.

Soy Sauce and Kecap Manis

Commercial soy sauces and the thick, sweeter version, kecap manis, have a negative nutritional value because many are not made with soy beans. The contents are hydrolized vegetable protein, caramel, colouring, a large amount of salt and water. Try not to use.

Tamari

The name also used by some producers of Nama Shoyu sauce, (see *above*). Check the labels carefully for additives.

Tempeh

This fermented soy product contains large amounts of iron and zinc, protein and vitamin B12. The craft of tempeh making most probably originated in Java and, together with the 'secret' ingredient that causes the tempeh to ferment and solidify, recipes are handed down through generations.
How to use: See recipes Bali.
Buy: From health food shops and Asian grocers in different

sized blocks. Really fresh tempeh can be frozen for 6 mths.
Substitute: Tofu.

Tofu

Made from soy milk, it comes in either a soft, firm or silken form. Although bland, it is nutritious and versatile.
How to use: Drain well before cutting into small cubes. Marinate in soy, ginger or other spices to absorb flavours. Add to soups and salads or puree to make thick salad dressings or sweet sauces.
Buy: Source tofu that has not been preserved with formaldehyde from health food shops or Asian grocers.

Spice Pastes

• Commercial, ready-made Asian spice pastes are available in many supermarkets. Only a few brands do not have additives, large amounts of salt or MSG and a whole list of preservatives, so check the labels carefully.
• Commercial spice pastes cannot be used for 'living' dishes because they have been heated during processing.
• If possible, buy fresh ingredients and take the time to make the fresh, healthy pastes and dressing recipes included in this book, adjusting the flavours to your taste!

Spices

Fresh spices are one of the essential ingredients in many SE-Asian cuisines. When 'translating' recipes for cooked spice pastes into 'living' uncooked recipes, it is important to keep tasting. Many spices develop more intensive flavours when cooked, so 'living' recipes have to be more carefully balanced.

Tips for storing spices:
• Try to buy fresh spices, not commercially-packed ground ones. Buy a coffee grinder to use solely for this purpose.
• Dried spices have to be kept in airtight glass jars a cool, dark place after opening. Throw away after a month or two.
• After using dried spices, replace lids at once.
• Always try to make your own spice mixtures and keep them either in the freezer or in airtight glass jars in a cool, dark cupboard.
• Note the date on any spice mixtures you make.
• Only buy small amounts so that the spices are fresh.
• Keep spices away from heat, moisture or sunlight.

Cardamon *lat. Elettaria cardomomum*

Used rarely in SE-Asian cuisine, but can add an Indian or Arabic flavour to different dishes.
How to use: Open the pods and take out the tiny seeds before blending or grinding.
Buy: Indian grocers or good supermarkets.

Cassia *lat. Cinnamomum cassia*

Used in SE-Asian spice mixtures, it is often confused with 'real' cinnamon *lat. Cinnamomum verum*, although cassia bark has a different flavour.
How to use: Buy some fresh 'quills', break into small pieces and blend into a powder in a spice (or coffee) mill.

Chilli *lat. Capsicum*

A few chilli species were among the many varieties of plants brought back to Europe by Christopher Columbus in the 15th century. Setting out towards the west, the reason for his voyage was primarily to find the illusive and mysterious Spice Islands, break the monopoly of the spice traders in Venice and discover new suppliers for silk and opium. Chillies had already been domesticated and eaten in South America for more than 6000 years. When Portuguese traders brought chillies to Europe for the first time, they also introduced them to India, Africa and Thailand. Chilli cultivation spread to China and other SE-Asian countries, becoming the most inexpensive and easy to grow spice in the world! Eating chillies on a regular basis provides many nutrients, vitamins and powerful antioxidants. Capsaicin is an antibiotic and boosts the immune system. Slightly addictive, chillies also stimulate the brain to release a pleasure stimulus – feeling good is part of the enjoyment. Many different varieties of chillies grow across the region, from tiny, really hot ones to the large milder red chillies.
How to buy: Only buy unwrinkled chillies that are not blemished. Smooth-skinned fresh chillies are hotter than the wrinkled ones.
Using dried chillies: Do not keep longer than two months or the heat and flavour will disappear. Cut with kitchen scissors and soak in hot water for about 1 hour to soften.
How to store: Wrap in newspaper and store in a plastic container in the fridge. Use quickly.
Buy: From Asian grocers or good supermarkets. Experiment with different kinds of chillies to find the ones you prefer.

Chinese Keys *lat. Kaempferia pandurata Roxb.*

This fragrant rhizome is used for Chinese medicine and spice pastes in Thailand and other parts of the region.
How to use: Remove the brown skin with a potato peeler, slice into small pieces and blend or pound with other spices.
Buy: Fresh from Thai or Asian grocers.

Cloves *lat. Syzygium aromaticum*

Originally grewn only on the Maluku Islands in Indonesia they were traded by Arabs until the Portugese discovered the source and took over the trade in the 15th century. An important ingredient in European cuisine during the Middle Ages, cloves are now used more in Indian and Arabic spice mixtures. They are anti-parasitic, boost the immune system and aid digestive problems.
How to use: Add 1 or 2 cloves to spice mixtures. Use sparingly as they have a very intense flavour.
Buy: Small batches of fresh whole cloves.

Coriander *lat. Coriandrum sativum*

The ground seeds used in many SE-Asian spice mixtures have a tangy, heady aroma different from the leaves or the more intensely flavoured roots. A natural antibiotic, the spice stimulates the appetite and relieves stomach disorders.
How to store: Sealed container in dark cupboard for less than 6 months.

How to use: Grind fresh seeds in a coffee mill or pestle and mortar.
Buy: Small amounts of fresh seeds.

Cumin *lat. Cuminum cyminum*

Is an ancient spice, with a distinctive, nutty flavour. Rich in iron and helpful in digestive problems, it is the second most important spice in the world after pepper.
How to use: Grind fresh seeds in a coffee mill or a pestle and mortar.
Buy: Small amounts as needed.

Five Spice Powder

This spice mixture is Chinese in origin, but is also used in many Vietnamese and some Thai dishes.
How to use: Add sparingly to sauces and dressings. Always make your own mixture from fresh, whole spices and adjust to your taste. Blend the following together in a spice mill. Keep in a tightly closed jar in a dark place and use within 3 months.
Recipe: 2tbs each cinnamon, dried ginger, star aniseed, fennel seeds, 1-2 fresh cloves, 1tsp black peppercorns, 1tsp Lao or Szechuan pepper.

Galangal *lat. Languas galangal*

One of the main spices in SE-Asian cuisine. This large rhizome can be kept for a time in a plastic bag in the fridge.
How to use: Scrape or peel off the skin, chop or slice then pound or blend into a paste with other ingredients.
Buy: Asian grocers or good supermarkets. Buy roots that look fresh and are not dry and do not buy powdered or dried galangal because it quickly looses its flavour.

Garlic

This member of the *allium* family is an indispensable and versatile ingredient along with ginger and Asian shallots, for all SE-Asian cuisines.
How to use: Chop finely to add to sauces and dressings or pound together with other ingredients into a spice paste. Store in a dark, cool and airy place.
Buy: Try to buy unblemished, closed bulbs that are firm to the touch.

Ginger *lat. Zingiber officinale*

This important culinary and medicinal herb is used extensively throughout the region.
How to use: Scrape off the skin using the tip of a teaspoon. Chop, grate or blend with other spices such as garlic and sea salt to make a basic paste to add to sauces, soups and dressings.
Tip: Fresh ginger 'hands' bend easily and have a smooth, pale brown skin. Candied or crystallized ginger have been heated and processed, so cannot be substituted for 'living' food preparation.
Buy: Asian grocers or good supermarkets.

Kencur *lat. Kaempferia galanga*

The tiny, fragrant rhizome is a relative of the ginger family

used mainly in Indonesian, Singaporean and Malaysian cuisines. Over the years it has had many different and confusing names, so I use the original Indonesian name.
How to use: Fresh kencur does not need to be peeled. Chop or slice prior to pounding or grinding into a paste to add to sauces or dressings.
Buy: Indonesian or Asian grocers.
Substitute: Fresh galangal.

Nutmeg and Mace *lat. Myristaca fragrans*
One of the spices that changed world history. Indigenous to the Maluku Islands in Indonesia, nutmegs are coated with a bright red mace filament that turns light brown and becomes brittle when dry.
How to use: Always buy fresh nutmegs and grate them when needed. Blades of mace can be ground or blended and added to spice mixes.
Book Tip: Nathaniel's Nutmeg: Or, The True and Incredible Adventures of the Spice Trader who Changed the Course of History by Giles Milton. Different editions available.

Pepper
Originally grown in India and Indonesia, the most used spice worldwide has influenced history and the global economy from the 10th century onwards. This extremely versatile spice is also known to stimulate the appetite.
How to use: Only buy whole peppercorns and grind as needed to keep the taste and flavour.

Pepper, Black *lat. Piper nigrum*
Fresh green peppercorns fermented and dried, shrivel and turn black during processing.

Pepper, Cubeb or Comet Tail *lat. Cubebe*
This type has recently become difficult to find even in its native Indonesia. The small, brownish coloured berries have a short tail and a bitter, pungent taste, ideal for spice pastes and dressings.
How to use: Combine with other peppercorns. Grind and add to sauces or dressings.
Buy: Specialist spice shops or online.

Pepper, Green *lat. Piper nigrum*
Young black pepper! Asian grocers sometimes sell fresh sprigs but usually green peppercorns are sold pickled in brine or vinegar in small jars. Fresh peppercorns are readily available at local markets in Thailand.
How to use: Crush and add to sauces or dressings or add some whole ones to salads or soups.
Buy: Asian grocers or good supermarkets.

Pepper, Long *lat. Piper longum*
This long, thin peppercorn was used extensively in Roman times. It is not well-known in the west and is difficult to find outside India and Indonesia.
How to use: Crush and add to spice blends and pastes.
Buy: Specialist spice shops or internet.

Pink Peppercorns *lat. Schinus terebinthifolius*
Native to South America these decorative pink berries come from the baies rose plant.
How to use: Crush and add sparingly to soups, sauces, dressings and salads.
Buy: Good supermarkets sell brine-packed or freeze-dried berries.

Szechuan or Lao Pepper *lat. Zanthoxylum piperitum*
This is not a member of the pepper family, but seeds of a berry from the prickly ash tree. Used in many spice mixtures, it has a very pungent and slightly lemony flavour.
How to use: Add sparingly to sauces, soups and dressings.
Buy: Specialist spice shops, Asian grocers or online.

White Pepper
Comes from black peppercorns soaked in water until the outer husk rots and can be removed. It has a milder taste than black peppercorns.

Salt *lat. Sodium chloride*
Commercial salt is whitened using chemicals, so sea or crystal mountain salts, the minerals still intact, are always best. Mix these natural salts with different kinds of peppers, zitrus zests or chillies for more unusual tastes. The media preaches that consuming too much salt is bad for our health because so much salt is added to all processed food. If we change to eating fresh, unprocessed foods, there is longer a problem!
Note: Using only natural salts can cause iodine deficiency and thyroid problems, so eat sea vegetables regularly.
Buy: Delicatessens, Asian grocers or online.
Book Tip: Salt, a World History, Mark Kurlansky, Vintage Press 2003

Star Aniseed *lat. Ilicium verum*
One of the most used spices in Chinese cuisine and an important ingredient in the Chinese Five Spice Powder.
How to use: Grind whole 'stars' in a coffee grinder. Use sparingly, the flavour is very intense.
Buy: Asian or Chinese grocers.

Turmeric *lat. Curcuma domestica*
Already mentioned in Assyrian herbals, bright yellow turmeric is important throughout SE-Asia – in the kitchen, in the preparation of traditional herbal remedies and as a colouring agent.
How to use: Scrape away the skin under running water and chop finely. Pound or grind to a paste to use with other ingredients. Be careful as turmeric stains are impossible to remove.
Buy: Try to find fresh turmeric at Asian grocers. Powdered alternatives have no flavour.

Sweeteners
Every kind of commercial sugar has been processed at high temperatures. Even the so-called 'raw' sugars sometimes have brown dyes added to make them look more natural!

Palm Sugar

Made from either the coconut or Palmyra palm (*lat. Borassus sundaica*), depending on area, it is a traditional sweetener produced by small farmers all over the region. Used to balance flavours in both sweet and savoury dishes, palm sugar is actually not a 'living food' because palm sap is boiled once to evaporate the water. However, because processing is limited, palm sugar is a healthier alternative and has antiseptic and anti-bacterial properties. Readily available throughout SE-Asia, it is, with raw honey, the main sweetener used in all the recipes in this book.

How to use: Palm sugar keeps for a long time in a container in the fridge. Grate or cut off chunks and blend with other ingredients as needed.

Recipe for 'living' palm sugar syrup: Grate 3 tbs palm sugar and add 1 tbs water or coconut water and a little vanilla to make a healthy 'living' syrup. Add to juices, desserts or salad dressings.

Buy: Asian grocers usually sell a wide selection of palm sugars, also called 'jaggery' in Indian shops. Buy different varieties and experiment until you find one you prefer.

Rock Sugar

Sold in 'rocks' mainly in Vietnam, and made from processed white and 'brown' sugar and sometimes honey, these are not to be confused with palm sugar.

Stevia *lat. Stevia rebaudiana*

There are hundreds of varieties of this plant originating from South America and now cultivated in some parts of SE-Asia. Usually sold in powder form, some varieties can be more than 200 times sweeter than sugar. Stevia has no calories so is an ideal sweetener for diabetics. It has a strange metallic aftertaste and, because it is so sweet, use sparingly, experiment and adjust recipes accordingly.

Buy: health food shops or online.

Sugar Cane *lat. Saccharum*

The sugar comes from the stem of the bamboo sugar cane, a variety of grass that grows mainly in Brazil and SE-Asia.

How to use: Peel off the outside layers down to the inner core, eat raw or use for sweetening desserts, dressings and juices.

Buy: Fresh from Asian grocers.

Vanilla Beans *lat. Vanilla fragrans*

The beans are picked while still green and dried in the sun. Always buy beans because many of the extracts (semi-dried beans are put into alcohol to extract the flavour) or powders have many additives or are completely artificial.

How to use: Most recipes require the inside of the bean to be scraped out. When making blender juices and sauces, I use the whole bean just trimming off each end before using.

Tea

Green Tea *lat. Camellia sinensis*

Tea is the dried leaves of this plant, cultivated in China and Japan. Processing is minimal, so the leaves contain a high level of anti-oxidants, reduce cholesterol and have many other health-giving properties.

Tip: Always take some to drink when flying. Drinking green tea helps to stop the formation of blood clots.

Buy: Only buy the best Japanese or Chinese green tea from well-known dealers or online.

Herbal Teas

These are the leaves of plants, herbs or edible flowers that do not belong to the tea plant family. Herbal teas have been used for medicinal purposes all over the world for thousands of years. Each country in SE-Asia also has its own special varieties of herbal teas.

How to use: Steep the leaves or edible flowers in hot water for 10 minutes, strain and drink. Soak leaves or flowers in warm water and drain well before adding to soups and salads. Store in an airtight container in a cool, dark place and use quickly once opened.

Buy: In small amounts from tea shops online, good supermarkets or Asian grocers. Always check the labels and sell by dates.

Tea Leaves, Pickled (see *Tasty Extras*).

Vegetable Stock Powder

Commercial vegetable stock powders contain huge amounts of salt and MSG. Using a dehydrator, make your own and balance the flavours according to your taste.

How to make: Wash leftover herbs and vegetables such as carrots, leeks, broccoli, cauliflower, dry and chop finely or use the vegetable pulp from juicing. Adjust the flavour and dehydrate in layers until crispy. Blend in a spice or coffee grinder. Make small batches and use quickly.

Vegetables

Among the most nutritious foods on the planet, they alkalize the blood, are full of calcium, chlorophyll and contain all the important nutrients needed to fuel the body everyday. Also see *Edible Leaves above*.

How to use: Many can be eaten raw but to make greens or beans more digestible, steam lightly before serving.

Shopping:
• Try to source only 'organically' grown vegetables.
• Never buy damaged or discoloured vegetables.
• If only frozen vegetables are available, check the packing date, the small print and remember that many of these have also been heat or chem-ically processed before freezing.
• Never buy damaged frozen packs or those full of ice; these have thawed and been refrozen.

Cleaning:
To reduce the risk of consuming compost or bacteria residues when eating organic raw fruit and vegetables, here are some guidelines for cleaning produce:
• Clean thoroughly just before using.
• Soak vegetables for 5 mins in bottled or distilled water. Vegetables or fruit with high water content should be carefully sprayed or rinsed.
• Sprinkle with baking soda then rinse off with water.
• Wash in a mixture of apple cider vinegar and spring water and scrub if necessary.

• Marinate in lemon juice to remove toxins. Dry carefully.
• Although vegetables may look clean and are labeled as
washed, wash again just to make sure, especially for
vegetables to be eaten raw.

Asian Red Onions lat. Allium family
Use only small, sweet-tasting purple onions to make Asian
dishes and spice pastes. Western shallots have a much
sharper taste unsuitable for the 'living' recipes in this book.
How to use: Peel off outer skin and chop or slice.
Buy: Asian grocers.

Asparagus lat. Asparagus officinalis
Thin, green-stemmed asparagus is cultivated in Thailand
and widely used across the region. A culinary ingredient
since Egyptian times, it is a diuretic, contains Vitamin C and
many vital nutrients.
How to buy: Check the base of the cut stems and do not buy
if dry and brittle. Peel woody bits from the stem with a
potato peeler and slice off the base. Do not peel young
asparagus.
Buy: Asian grocers or good supermarkets.

Aubergine or Egg Plant lat. Solanum family
Found growing wild or cultivated in all shapes, sizes and
colours across the region.
How to use: Small Asian eggplants can be sliced and used raw.
Older ones or larger varieties should be sliced thinly,
sprinkled with salt, left for 30 mins before rinsing with
water and drying carefully.
Buy: Asian grocers.
Substitute: Any small, fresh eggplants from supermarkets or
farmers' markets.

Baby Corn lat. Zea mays
Sweet young corn is used whole or sliced in all kinds of
soups and salads.
Buy: Fresh at good supermarkets and Asian grocers.

Bamboo Shoots lat. Phyllostachus, bambusa or dendrocalamus
Just two of the many varieties of bamboo that grow
throughout the region.
How to use: Young bamboo shoots are boiled before using.
Only the tiniest young shoots can be used for 'living' food.
Trim away the base and the outer leaves and use only the
soft inner core.
Buy: Fresh at Asian grocers. Never buy the tinned shoots
because they have been heat processed.

Beans lat. leguminosae family
Many different varieties of beans have been eaten as a staple
all over the world for over 7,000 years. There are two main
types: the pod form and mature beans taken out of the pod
and usually sold dried. In Bali the small, red adzuki beans
are used for soup or raw in a sambal, green beans are
served in a raw salad all over Indonesia and green 'yard
long' beans are available all over the region.

Beans, Dried see Sprouts.
How to use: Never try to eat raw but soak and sprout before
using.

Beans, Long or Beans, Long Yard lat. Vigna unguiculata
Used all over SE-Asia and often cultivated between the rice
paddies.
How to use: Buy only firm, bright green beans. Wash well
and cut into tiny rounds to add to soups and salads.
Alternatively slice and steam gently until just tender.
Buy: Asian grocers.

Beans, Winged lat. Psophocarpus tetragonolobus
Rich in protein they add an interesting visual aspect to
'raw' dishes.
How to use: Choose only the youngest, bright green beans,
cut off the strings along the 'wings' and slice finely or slice
and steam gently until just tender.
Buy: Asian grocers.

Bitter Gourd lat. Momordica charantia
Only the smallest, youngest green gourds can be eaten raw.
Shaped like a cucumber, they have a very knobbly green
skin and contain more nutrients and vitamins than many
other green vegetables.
How to use: Slice finely and soak in spring water with 1 tsp.
salt for 30 minutes. Drain well and use sparingly. Or slice
very thinly and steam gently until just tender, (see Cambodia).
Buy: Asian or Indian grocers.

Bok Choy (see Herbs & Edible Leaves).

Broccoli lat. Brassicaceae family
Originating in Europe, broccoli has been a favourite
vegetable in Italy for thousands of years. Rich in vitamin C
it has anti-cancer and anti-bacterial properties.
How to use: Buy only bright green 'heads'. Slice them finely
and use for salads, in vegetable 'noodle' dishes or soups.
Peel the stems, shred for salads or blend for juices.
Alternatively slice stems and steam gently until just tender.
Buy: Try to buy only 'organically' grown broccoli, rinse well
to remove insects before using.

Cabbage lat. Brassia cultivars
Many different varieties have been grown all over the world
for thousands of years. The white round cabbage and long
Chinese leaves are a favourite all over SE-Asia.
How to use: Remove the tough outer leaves and shred finely.
Salt sliced cabbage in warm salty water for 20 mins then
drain before using or steam until just tender.

Cauliflower lat. Brassica oleracea
A favourite vegetable used in Chinese influenced dishes all
over SE-Asia.
How to use: Soak in salted water to remove insects. Chop or
slice finely and add to soups or salads. Chop the stems and
use raw or steam lightly until just tender.

Carrots lat. *Daucus carota subsp. Sativus*
Carrots are used in all SE-Asian countries. Rich in vitamin
A, anti-oxidants and a source of beta carotine, purple,
yellow, white and orange varieties of carrots are most
nutritious when eaten raw.
How to use: Buy loose, 'organic' carrots if possible, wash well
and peel to remove any bacteria.

Chayote or Choko lat. *sechium edule* originally came from
Mexico. Rich in amino acids and vitamin C, the roots,
leaves, tendrils and seeds of this trailing vine are edible as
are the pear-shaped green vegetables.
How to use: Buy smaller, tender chayote. Peel and slice finely,
washing off the sticky white sap. Use for soups, salads and
juices.
Buy: Asian grocers and good supermarkets.

Cucumber lat. *Cucumis sativus*
Cucumber and others in the squash, gourd and melon
family are some of the world's oldest recorded vegetables.
How to use: If the skin is tough, peel it off. Always scrape off
and discard indigestible seeds.

Daikon lat. *Raphanus sativus*
Sweet and crunchy when fresh, this large white radish is a
very versatile addition to salads and soups. It is diuretic,
helps eliminate mucus in the body, contains many digestive
enzymes, is antifungal and inhibits the growth of cancer.
How to use: Always buy with head and leaves intact.
Buy: Asian and Japanese grocers.

Jicama or Yam lat. *Pachyrhizus erosus*
A large tuber with beige skin and crunchy white flesh.
How to use: Wash well, peel and slice or grate. Add to salads
or soups.
Buy: Asian grocers.

Kailan lat. *Brassica oleracea*
Finely chop the thin broccoli-like stalks and dark green
leaves for salads and soups. Broccoli can be used as an
alternative. Steam until just tender if preferred.
Buy: Asian grocers.

Leek lat. *Allium ampeloprasum var. porrum*
Small, thin leeks are available across SE-Asia.
How to use: Remove the woody outer leaves and slice the
inner ones very finely. To use in 'living' cuisine, soak sliced
leeks in water with added salt to make the flavour milder or
steam until just tender.

Lotus Root lat. *Nelumbo nucifera*
Has a light brown skin with firm, white flesh.
How to use: Peel and slice very thinly. Use for decoration or
add to soups and salads.
Buy: Asian or Chinese grocers.

Mushrooms
Those listed below are cultivated and readily available in

most parts of the region. As the only vegetables that provide
a natural source of Vitamin D, they are an important health
food for people living in less sunnier climes.
How to buy and store fresh mushrooms:
• Only buy fresh mushrooms that are not slimy, too wet or
too dry.
• Mushrooms with open caps have more flavour than those
with closed ones.
• Buy small quantities as needed and use at once.
• Remove from any plastic packaging, separate and keep in
a brown paper bag if possible.
• Keep cool and dry.
• Rinse quickly under running water, dip in lemon or lime
juice to destroy any insects then pat dry just before using.
• Never freeze fresh mushrooms.
How to store and use dried mushrooms:
• Buy small packets and use quickly as required.
• Store opened packets in airtight containers in the dark.
• Ensure that the dried mushrooms look fresh, not broken
or faded.
• Soak for 10 mins before using and change the water a few
times. Discard water after soaking.

Mushrooms, Button lat. *Garicus bisporus*
Readily available and versatile.
How to use: Wash & dry carefully and cut off the base of
the stem. Sprinkle with lime or lemon juice to stop discolouration. Chop or slice before adding to soups or salads.

Mushrooms, Cloud Ear lat. *Auricularia polytricha*
A rubbery, fungus often used in Chinese or Thai cuisine.
How to use: Cut off the woody stems, soak until soft. Pat dry
and discard the water. Chop and use for soups or salads.
Buy: Rarely available fresh, buy dried fungus from Asian
grocers or good supermarkets.

Mushrooms Enoki lat. *Flammulina velutipes* have tiny caps and
long stems. Used mostly in Thai and Chinese dishes, they
are grown across the region.
How to use: Chop the stems and add to pastes or dressings.
Use the tiny caps in salads and soups.
Buy: Asian grocers or good supermarkets.

Mushrooms, Oyster lat. *Pleurotus ostreatus*
This pale, fan-shaped mushroom is grown commercially in
most Asian countries.
How to use: Clean carefully and sprinkle with lime or lemon
juice after chopping or slicing.
Buy: Good supermarkets.

Mushrooms, Shiitake lat. *Lentinula edodes*
Always an important ingredient in Chinese and Japanese
cuisine, they are now readily available everywhere.
How to use: The fresh mushrooms have a 'meaty' taste and
sliced or chopped, can be added to soups and salads. Dried
mushrooms have a more intense flavour and should be
soaked for 20 mins and the water discarded before use.
Buy: Asian or Japanese grocers and supermarkets.

Mushrooms, Straw lat.*Volvariella volvacea*
Mushrooms are widely used in Thailand and SE-Asia.
How to use: Wash fresh mushrooms carefully and discard the woody part of the stems.
Buy: Only buy fresh mushrooms, canned ones have no flavour at all and can have a slimy texture.

Mustard Greens lat.*Brassica juncea*
Used widely in SE-Asia because they are inexpensive and full of nutrients. Because of their mustard flavour, the seeds are used to make Dijon mustard.
How to use: Leaves are sold in bunches. Only buy fresh, green leaves, clean well, slice and chop, or slightly steam before adding to salads and soups.
Buy: Asian or Indian grocers.

Okra lat.*Abelmoschus esculentus*
A popular vegetable across Asia.
How to use: Only buy the small, tender, bright green okra, remove the stem and slice very finely. Add to soups and salads.
Buy: Indian or Asian grocers and supermarkets.

Palmhearts lat.*Cocos nucifera*
The innermost stem of coconut or similar palm trees.
How to use: Remove any woody outer skin. Cut into thin rounds and add to soups and salads.
Buy: Fresh from Asian grocers. Do not buy the tinned ones, these have been heat processed and have no flavour.

Peas lat.*Pisum sativum*
Readily available and widely used all over the region.
How to use: Shelled fresh peas are sweet. Sliced young snowpea and mangetout peapods can also be used. Remove stems and 'strings' from the sides of the pods, slice or steam if preferred.
Buy: Asian grocers and good supermarkets.

Pumpkin lat.*Cucurbitaceae family*
Many different varieties of pumpkins are grown all over the world and used widely in SE-Asia.
How to use: For 'living' food, make fine 'noodles' with a vegetable cutter, or grate (see *Utensils*) and soak for 20 mins in slightly salted water to soften, or steam before using.

Spinach, Green lat.*Amaranthus*
Grows wild all over SE-Asia. Has tougher, tastier leaves than European varieties. Loosing 50% of its vitamin C content very quickly, use immediately after buying in soups or salads.
How to use: Choose only dark green, unblemished leaves. Rinse well, steam if preferred or chop and add raw to soups and salads. Blend for juices.
Buy: Asian or Indian grocers.

Spinach, Red lat.*Amaranthus*
A favourite vegetable across Asia.
How to use: Puree for soups or use unblemished leaves in salads.
Buy: Asian or Indian grocers.

Sprouted Beans, Grains and Vegetables
Easy to grow at home they are digestible and nutritious. Although germination inhibits inherent toxicity, sprouts should only be eaten in moderation. Detailed instructions, and sprouting times for each variety are available online.

Tips for buying sprouts:
• Because eating commercial sprouts has sometimes caused outbreaks of salmonella, always try to grow your own from seed. This is very easy and enablesyou can control the purity of the water and only use them when they are really fresh.
• Try to source 'organic' sprouting seeds from reliable suppliers that have no pesticide residues.
• Only try to buy sprouts that look as fresh as possible. Always check the date on the packaging.
• Do not buy if the container has any brown water residue.
• Bought sprouts of any kind may contain bacteria. Rinsing solely with plain water may not remove these. For alternative methods, (see *Vegetables*).

Tomato lat.*Solanum lycopersicum*
Seeds were probably brought to Europe from South America by Cortez in the 16th century. The cultivation of tomatoes spread rapidly throughout the rest of the world and many different varieties are used in all SE-Asian cuisines. They are extremely versatile, contain many anti-oxidants and large amounts of vitamin A and C.

Water Chestnuts lat.*Eleocharis dulcis*
Adds a crunchy, sweet flavour to soups and salads.
How to use: Peel off the skin and use at once.
Buy: Chinese and Asian grocers and markets.

Waterspinach or Morning Glory
See *Herbs & Edible Leaves*.

Zucchini lat.*Cucurbita pepo*
This member of the squash family probably originated in South America and Italy. The flowers are edible once the stamens are removed.
How to use: Buy only the smallest young zucchini and slice or grate for use in soups and salads.

Water
If possible, use only pure mineral water in glass bottles for cooking to avoid traces of chemical residue in many 'food grade' plastic ones! To flush out toxins and avoid dehydration drink at least 2 litres of mineral water per day.

Wine
Made of fermented grapes, wine is fortunately a natural 'living' food. Many good organic, vegan wines, guaranteed free from animal additives such as egg whites, are now available. A glass of organic wine red every day or so has numerous health benefits.

Equipment & Utensils
'Living' food cuisine needs some special equipment. If you

are seriously considering adopting this way of eating for the future, make sure to buy the best you can afford. Websites of recommended manufacturers are listed under each machine. If buying on-line, shop around because prices can differ enormously from country to country.

Bamboo Sushi Mats
Used for all kinds of vegetable rolls are available at Asian and Japanese grocers.

Brushes
Buy natural brushes to scrub naturally grown fruit and vegetables.

Chopping Boards
Buy good quality, untreated, thick hardwood boards, not synthetic ones, with separate ones for onions, garlic and spices, for chopping salads and vegetables and one for fruit.

Citrus Juicer
Invest in an electrically powered one if you make large amounts of juice. For manufacturers, see Food Processor).

Coffee or Spice Grinder
This small gadget is inexpensive, easily replaceable and ideal for grinding dry spice mixtures or small amounts of spice pastes.

Cutters
All shapes and sizes are available at good kitchen shops. Make a collection and decorate plates for special occasions. Buy only metal ones for stability and long life.

Dehydrator
Removes moisture from fruit, vegetables and 'cooks' crackers and sweet things, while keeping the enzymes intact. Try using your kitchen oven at low temperatures and experiment before buying a good quality, expensive dehydrator. The dehydrator listed below is available in different sizes, is easy to use and the most reliable on the market. Make sure to order extra Teflex sheets to use on the removable trays. www.excaliburdehydrators.com
The supplier I use for Southeast Asia, is based in Australia: www.vitality4life.com

Food Processor
Using a processor everyday shortens the life and sharpness of the blades, so buy the best quality all-round machine. When purchasing, try to buy extra blades as long as replacements are available. Cuisinart: www.cuisinart.com
Krups: www.krups.com
Magimix: www.magimix.com

Glass Jars
Buy a selection of all shapes and sizes, for storage.

Ice Cream Maker
Not an absolute necessity but fun if you enjoy making imaginative sorbets and dairy-free ice creams. For manufacturers, (see *above*).

Ice Cube Trays
Those with lids are good for freezing ice cubes containing fresh, chopped fruit for decorative drinks.

Juicer
Invaluable for fruit and vegetable juices (reserve left over pulp to make dehydrated crackers, (see Tasty Extras). Suggested manufacturers above.

Kitchen Scissors
For snipping fresh herbs and dried chillies.

Knives
Invest in a set of good knives that feel comfortable in your hand and make sure that they are always sharp.

Mandoline
A quick and easy way to slice all kinds of fruit and vegetables finely. Many different sizes are available in every price range from good kitchen shops.
www.benriner.co.jp www.chefknifes.com

Nutmilk Bag
Available from health food and kitchen shops. Alternatively, put two layers of cheese-cloth inside a fine sieve.

Parisienne Ballers
Use to make perfect, decorative balls out of all kinds of fruit and vegetables. Available from good kitchen shops. www.fdick.com

Pestle & Mortar
The best ones are heavy ones of marble or lava. These are available in good kitchen shops or Asian grocers. With a little hard work and effort, spice pastes taste much better than those made in the blender.

Plastic containers
Good for keeping food fresh in the fridge. Buy only the best quality available. www.tupperware.com

Spatulas
For scraping pastes, powders and sauces out of difficult corners.

Spiral Slicer
Quickly turns all kinds of hard fruit and vegetables into different thicknesses of noodles. This German manufacturer always new and exciting products: www.lurch.de

Superblender
A high speed, power blender and the best of its kind. More effective and longer lasting than a traditional domestic blender, the chopping blades and turbo-charged engine can cope with making nutmilks and hard green vegetables.

Read the instruction manual carefully before using.
www.viitamix.com
www.vitality4life.com

Superjuicer

Does not cut ingredients but cold presses them with a gentle, slow turning screw action that leaves enzymes and nutrients intact. Juices wheatgrass and delicious banana ice cream made with fresh bananas straight from the freezer!
www.oscar-living-juicer.com www.championjuicer.com
www.samsonjuicers.com www.vitality4life.com

Zester

A uick and easy way of grating anything from citrus zest to nutmeg. Available at kitchen suppliers and good kitchen shops. www.us.microplane.com

Measuring Up

Because none of the recipes in this book use exact measurements,
the following can just be used as general guidelines:

Weight
Teaspoons (tsp) & Tablespoons (tbs)
5g = 1 teaspoon (tsp)
15g = 1 tablespoon (tbs) = 3 tsp = $^1/_2$ oz

Grams (g)to Pounds, Ounces (oz) and Cups
15g = $^1/_2$ oz
30g = 1 oz = $^1/_8$ cup
60g = 2 oz = $^1/_4$ cup
100g = 3.5 oz
120g = 4 oz = $^1/_2$ cup
175g = 6 oz = $^3/_4$ cup
200g = 7 oz
350g = 12 oz = 1 cup
450g = 1 pound (lb)
500g = 1 lb 2 oz
1000g (1 kg) = 2 lb 4 oz

Volume
Millilitres (ml) & Litres (l) to Fluid Ounces (fl oz) & Pints
15 ml = 1 tbs = 1 fl oz
150 ml = 5 fl oz = $^1/_4$ pint
300 ml = 10 fl oz = $^1/_2$ pint
450 ml = 14 fl oz = $^3/_4$ pint
600 ml = 20 fl oz = 1 pint
1000 ml = 1 liter = 1 pint 14 fl oz

Linear
Centimeters (cm) to Inches (in)
1 centimeter (cm) = $^1/_2$ inch (in)
2 cm = $^3/_4$ in
5 cm = 2 in
10 cm = 4 in

INDEX